Kinder Dolls

A WALDORF DOLL-MAKING HANDBOOK

Maricristin Sealey

Hawthorn Press

Published by Hawthorn Press, Hawthorn House, 1 Lansdown Lane, Stroud, Gloucestershire, GL5 1BJ, UK
Tel: (01453) 757040 Fax: (01453) 751138
hawthornpress@hawthornpress.com
www.hawthornpress.com

Illustrations by Isabel Sealey
Cover illustration by Isabel Sealey
Cover design by Patrick Roe, Southgate Solutions Ltd., Stroud, Gloucestershire
Book design and typesetting by Lynda Smith
Printed in the UK by The Bath Press, Bath

British Library Cataloguing in Publication Data applied for.

ISBN 1 903458 03 X

Contents

For Sarah, where it all began...

'A comprehensive guide to doll making. The best instructions for doing hair styles that I have seen.'

Judy Quick, Handwork Teacher

'In a world increasingly invaded by synthetic materials, the appealing form and the integrity of the materials used in the making of these dolls offer sensory nourishment to the child.

They awaken a positive emotional response and the loving effort involved in producing such a doll creates a bond between mother and child.'

Lynne Oldfield, Director, London Waldorf Early Years Training Course

Foreword

The special relationship between a child and her doll is dynamic, and often mysterious, as relationships are. It is about love and nurturing, friendship and ownership, the emergence of self, and the subtle expression of all that the child imbibes from the adults who surround her. It is personal, private, often intuitive, and as old as the first doll that ever found itself in the hands of a child. A doll frequently becomes a separate and important character in a child's life, and, for this reason, stands to be the most significant toy a child will ever own. It is in this 'sacred' space of a child's play with her doll, that a parent is sometimes privileged to witness the innocent and important emulating of adult behavior. What a treasure it was to quietly 'eavesdrop' upon my daughters' play, and find them nursing their babies and softly cooing to them, or listening to their wee voices console, scold, instruct or express delight in their charges. 'Oh, how lovely you look in your new dress!' 'Samantha, get down from that chandelier this instant!' And so on. It is as early as this that a child first learns and practices what it is to be a parent.

Before dolls were mass-produced, it would have been rare to find any two exactly alike. Dolls, like people, were individuals, and were often created with a particular individual in mind. Though there are some beautiful dolls on the market today, it is now rare to find a play doll that is wholly unique. A handcrafted doll is one-of-a-kind, an individual which carries the spirit of the maker in its stitches and absorbs the spirit of the child who loves it. It is a beautiful thing to craft a doll with your own hands, sew it together with love, then make a gift of it to your child with the words, 'I made this for you!' In an age of consumerism, children often grow up thinking that things just magically come from stores. They miss out on the process of something being made, of watching it develop out of nothing more than scraps of fabric and tiny stitches, inspiration and hard-work. What a gift we give to our children when we involve them in the making of things, even if their involvement is no more than that of curious onlooker. Not only do they see where something 'came from', but they can gain a sense of security in the knowledge that something can be made, that indeed they themselves could make it.

Maricristin's book is a fine source for the beginning doll-maker. It is a valuable primer, full of practical tips, simple designs and clear, easy-to-follow instructions. She includes a chapter on General Techniques, which covers explanations and advice on safety, basic tools and materials, (how to find them and how to use them), and basic sewing techniques. Here I particularly appreciated her suggestions for recycling materials that you might already have in the home, i.e. old T-shirts, woollen socks, etc. There are ten different doll patterns that range in difficulty from the basic First Project: A Tiny Baby Doll, to Limbed Dolls with removable clothing. She devotes an entire chapter to doll Hair, a topic of infinite possibilities and of great importance to little girls, that has been sorely overlooked in other texts. She also provides a great chapter on doll Clothing that includes 12 basic patterns, along with unique suggestions for fabric selection and embellishments.

But perhaps the loveliest aspect of this doll primer is the fact that it is authored and illustrated by a mother and daughter team. Isabel, age 18, illustrated the beautiful full-color cover, as well as the sketches and diagrams throughout the book. It is my pleasure to recommend this charming craft book to all aspiring doll-makers.

Sara McDonald, Magic Cabin Dolls

Introduction

I have chosen to call this book **Kinder Dolls** – because whether you read this with the English meaning as being gentler and softer or the German translation as 'children' – both the actual physical feel and the true nature of the dolls described here is conveyed. They are real 'child dolls' not because they mimic exactly the features and form of an individual as many of the tough plastic toys available today try to do, but because they reflect the inner softness and warmth both of their maker and of their owner.

Most of the dolls currently on sale are designed to appeal to adults and adult conceptions of childhood. In the most extreme cases bisque or china dolls are made exclusively for grown ups, being too fragile and expensive to be played with. The dolls I make, and have written about in this book, are the opposite of those fashion plate ornaments. They are dolls to be played with, to be dressed and washed, to become part of its owners every day life, to be a friend, a playmate and a confidante. They become more attractive with age, for any blemishes, worn patches or sparse hair do not detract from but rather enhance the individuality of the doll.

For a child, play is their work and just as a craftsman cannot achieve good results with inferior materials so children need toys with integrity if they are to find play satisfying.

Cloth dolls have long been loved by children, rag dolls have been found in the ancient tombs of Egypt and Peru, and in their simplest form of knotted or folded fabric are universal. Dolls are a reflection of ourselves – of our bodies, our attitudes and our dreams. They can be made from many mediums but should above all provide what a child needs rather than that which an adult considers appropriate.

The basic cloth doll has developed in different ways in different countries, such as the rag doll or 'Raggedy Anne' of the USA, more complex felt dolls made by Lenci, Steiff and Chad Valley in Europe and the painted cloth dolls of Kathe Kruse, but whenever a small amount of time and resources have been available mothers have raided their ragbags to make dolls for their children. This book follows on in the tradition of those mothers and I hope will help anyone who wants to make a doll for a child to play with.

These 'Kinder Dolls' are made from sheepswool and cotton knit fabric with an unique inner head which gives form but not detail to the face. The origins of this type of doll come from a strong European tradition of dollmaking. Germany was the leading doll manufacturer in Europe in the 19th and early 20th century, dominating the doll market at home and abroad. Many dolls and toys were made at home during the long winter months with materials that were at hand – wood, sheepswool and cloth scraps. Individual craftspeople, notably Kathe Kruse, then developed these simple toys into commercial enterprises and the products found a ready market amongst the increasingly prosperous countries of Europe and America. However, dolls still continued to be made at home and the simplicity and charm of these formed dolls stuffed with sheepswool ensured their survival despite the plethora of more sophisticated toys.

In Europe, and later America, this type of doll became known as a 'Waldorf Doll', and had a strong connection with Steiner Education. Communities and Schools, based on Rudolf Steiner's methods, were established in many different countries and the tradition of making this particular type of doll continued alongside the education. Simple toys made from natural material are recognised as being of great importance for the wholesome development of young children.

Often dolls were made by groups of parents and teachers who had had no formal training in making dolls. Existing dolls were copied and new ideas developed and the success of the project would be judged by watching the children play with the new dolls. I still work in this way.

I began dollmaking when the parents from my daughter's class were asked to make dolls and soft toys for a stall at the School's Christmas fair. We were a group of ten or so with a great deal of enthusiasm, varying amounts of sewing skills and very little knowledge. One or two people had made dolls for their own children, several of us consulted books, the handwork teacher at school donated sheepswool and we searched our cupboards and drawers for fabrics. Then we began.

At first we made simple stuffed dolls with round heads and floppy bodies. Everyone who saw these first creations greeted them with delight and amazement. Grown-ups were astonished that such simple shapes and colours could be so appealing and were impressed that **we had made them**. 'You did this yourself?' 'Who taught you?' And frequently 'Can you teach me?' The reaction from the children was much simpler; they reached out, hugged and held on. Not many of those first dolls made it to the fair!

This initial success was very satisfying and encouraged us to continue sewing. We made mistakes, found some shapes more pleasing than others, developed a 'feel' for colour,

improved our techniques and realised how much more we had to learn and how little time we had to meet the deadline of the Christmas Fair.

However, somehow, we managed to produce a stall full of dolls and toys. Those of us who had spent many long hours cutting out, stuffing and sewing and had neglected houses and calloused fingers to prove it, were well rewarded by all the positive comments and also the money raised for our school.

When the dust had settled and the last piece of Christmas cake had been eaten, a few members of the original group decided that we would 'do it again', but this time we would start earlier, be more organised and try to build on our success. We met one morning a week, during term time, at one person's house. We brought our babies and toddlers, shared coffee, juice and cakes, and amidst the gentle chaos we sewed and chatted. We helped and encouraged each other and whenever we could we enlarged our knowledge.

One German-speaking mother went to Switzerland, and came back full of excitement because she learned a new way of sewing on hair. Another friend visited her family in Israel and came back with several metres of chocolate brown cotton knit – exactly the right colour for a group of ethnic dolls. A Swedish family sent a beautifully illustrated dollbook from their country. We couldn't understand a word of the text but the patterns and illustrations were so clear it didn't matter. Several people went through their children's dolls and found new models to copy and adapt. A very generous and gifted artist showed us how to make stunning silk string puppets.

The more dolls we made the better they turned out and the more we wanted to continue sewing. We found our own children were our best admirers and our hardest critics, and they often had strong ideas of how they wanted their dolls to look. I developed the pattern for the jointed dolls whilst expecting my third child because my daughters clamoured for 'a real baby that wears proper clothes and we can put a nappy on'.

The doll group has been in existence now for more than ten years and most of the original members have moved on but others have come to take their places. I have stayed and now find myself as the leader because of my many years of experience and the hundreds of dolls I have made. My own children are now almost past the doll playing age, although my oldest daughter still has her baby doll by her bed. Rosie was made to celebrate the birth of my third child who is now twelve years old. Rosie has some hair missing, her stuffing is a little lumpy from repeated washings and she doesn't get her clothes changed too often these days but she still has her place at the heart of my daughter's room. This is my real motivation for making dolls and teaching others to be able to do the same.

Of course dollmaking is an art, not an exact science, so the dolls made in different countries and by different people were not identical, but the essential being was maintained. The dolls I make are part of the British tradition; while still easily identifiable as 'Waldorf Dolls' they have their own individual characteristics being, for instance, softer than many German dolls and rounder than dolls made in Sweden. I prefer to make dolls with soft hair that can be styled in lots of different ways whereas others may prefer sewn on or embroidered hair.

I have developed the descriptions and patterns in this book over many years of making and teaching people how to make Waldorf dolls, but they still follow the same principles as dolls made in many parts of the world. I enjoy playing a part in that dollmaking tradition and I hope you will join me in creating these distinctive dolls, for your own pleasure, and for the children in your life.

Maricristin Sealey

How to use this book

The projects in this book are arranged in order of difficulty. The soft dolls in the earlier chapters on **Small Dolls** and **Soft Dolls** include full size drawings to compare with your work and some of the very basic steps are explained in great detail. They are also much quicker to complete than the limbed dolls.

None of the dolls require advanced skills but, if you have never worked with sheepswool or cotton knit fabrics before, it would be sensible to start with a small project before progressing to making a limbed doll.

A good plan of work would be to start with the **tiny baby** in the First Project, continue by making a **pouch** or **angel doll** from the Small Dolls chapter and then a **baggy doll** as explained in the chapter on Soft Dolls before choosing a **limbed** or **jointed doll** to sew.

It is essential to read the chapter on **General Techniques**, which contains much important information and advice, before beginning to make any of the dolls.

A First Project

Tiny baby doll

This tiny doll is quick to make and perfect for small hands to hold. It can be made from scraps of material and stuffed with sheepswool gleaned from hedgerows, or even little pieces of shredded knitting wool.

I make dozens of these every year, to sell at school fairs and to give as presents. They are perfect to find at the bottom of a Christmas stocking or nestling in the pocket of a new dress. I love to see children, big and little walking round with this very simple baby in their hands. It is small enough to be hidden in a school bag or placed in its very own tiny drawstring bag and hung in a place of honour from a dress or coat.

A three year old was given a family of five of these tiny babies and she insisted that they should inhabit the heirloom dolls house owned by her older siblings. Soon all the more sophisticated miniature dolls were relegated to a shoe box and the house was 'taken over' by the soft dolls, who were able to live in luxury in a three storey house. I showed the family how to make more babies and they made lots of them in different shades of blues, reds and pastels. Each colour family lived on a separate floor and intricate games and stories were woven around their daily lives. These tiny dolls were the instigators of hours of creative imaginative play for the whole family.

Young children can make these tiny baby dolls, with a little help from an adult or older sibling. I have made them successfully at my five year old's birthday party where the project provided both an enjoyable activity and also a charming gift to take home.

To speed matters along, I cut the circles of cotton knit and cut and machine sewed the fabric bodies before starting to work with the children. It's also important to have a finished model so everyone can see what they are going to achieve.

The drawings are all shown actual size, so you can compare your work directly with the pictures at each stage to check everything is progressing correctly.

Materials
Circle of flesh-coloured, cotton knit fabric, or stretchy T-shirt material
Scrap of soft fabric for the body – e.g. velour, brushed cotton or stretch toweling
Sewing thread to match body fabric
Small quantity of soft filling: e.g. teased sheepswool, shredded knitting yarn etc.
Optional: coloured pencil or sewing thread for eyes, small length of wool for hair

Instructions
1. Trace the patterns given on the next page and use them to cut out a head and a body from appropriate fabrics.

The body pattern is placed with the straight edge on the fold of the material, with the grain of the fabric going down the length of the body.

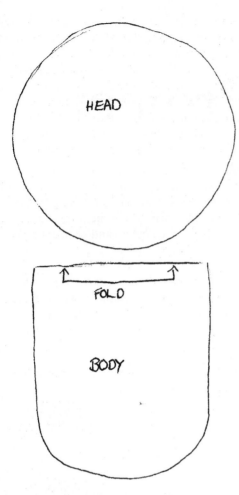

HEAD

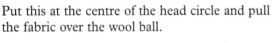

FOLD

BODY

Make sure the head is quite hard. If you have lots of creases at the neck then more wool is needed.

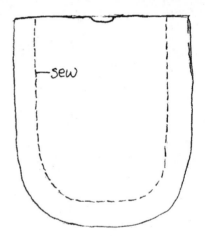

neck

You will now have a rounded head with fabric hanging down below the neck. Tie with strong sewing thread.

3. With the right sides of the fabric together, machine or hand sew round the open edges of the folded body piece.

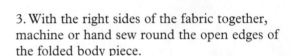

sew

2. To make the head, take a small piece of carded sheepswool and roll between the palms of your hands so that you have a hard ball of wool about the size of a marble (³/₄″ [1.5cm]).

Put this at the centre of the head circle and pull the fabric over the wool ball.

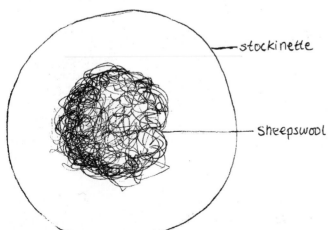

stockinette

sheepswool

Cut a small hole at the centre of the body, and turn the fabric so the right sides are outside. Stuff lightly.

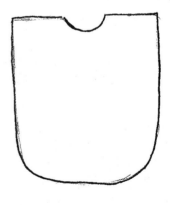

4. Thread a needle with sewing cotton to match the body fabric. Start at the middle of the neck edge at the back and sew a running stitch around the neck, turning in the raw edge as you go. This means you

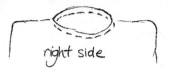

will be sewing through two thickness of fabric. Do not fasten off this thread until the head has been put in.

5. Place the excess fabric hanging down from the head inside the body. Pull up the gathering thread snugly around the neck and then sew the head to the body with small stitches.

Optional: eyes and hair

This tiny doll is quite sweet without any further features but if you want to add more details then keep them very simple.

Eyes

Two small dots are plenty to give lots of expression to the face. Use the drawing as a guide for the position of the eyes.

The simplest way to mark the eyes is with a coloured pencil – the colour will fade over time but can easily be renewed. Put two dots of colour on the face about half way down.

A more permanent method is to sew two small stitches with sewing thread. Mark the position of the eyes with a pencil dot. Start your thread at the back of the head where the head and body meet, bring the needle through the head to the first eye and take a small stitch, make another stitch for the second eye. Bring the needle back through the head to the starting position and then finish off with a stitch.

Hair

Cut a few pieces of wool 1″ (2.5cm) long and sew, with matching sewing thread, to the top of the head. Tease out or unravel the strands of wool to give a fluffy topknot.

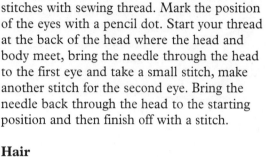

or

Thread a needle with embroidery thread or knitting wool and sew a few straight stitches across the top of the head. Start and finish the yarn with a french knot.

A small container, some scraps of fabric and a little sheepswool will make a snug bed for this baby.

A first doll

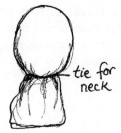

This is a very simple doll based on a square of fabric. The points of the hat and hands are knotted and are good for a baby to chew on. The doll can be washed in the machine, on a wool or delicates programme.

Make several of these dolls in a smaller size and sew or tie the hands together. Suspend the row of dolls where baby can see and touch to make an attractive pram or cot toy.

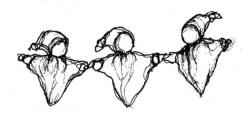

Materials

Soft, stretchy fabric such as cotton knit or towelling in the following sizes:
Body: 14″ x 14″ (36cm x 36cm))
Hat: 10″ x 8″ (25cm x 20cm)
Cotton gauze tubing 2″ (5cm) wide and 8″ (20cm) long
or
8″ (20cm) circle of cotton knit
Strong thread or crochet cotton
2oz (50gm) sheepswool
Optional: small bell

To make the doll

Head

1. From tubing
Tie the tubing together at one end.

Turn, so the knot and raw edges are inside.

Stuff the tube with the sheepswool to get a ball shaped inner head about 2½″ (7.5cm) high and 8″ (20cm) in diameter. Tie firmly at the bottom or neck.

2. From cotton knit

Mould the sheepswool into a round ball and place at the centre of the circle of cotton knit. Gather the fabric around the fleece ball and tie at the base for neck.

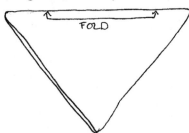

Body

1. Fold the square of fabric diagonally, with right sides together, so that you have a triangle.

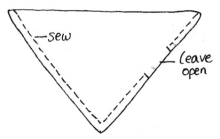

2. Sew the two sides of the triangle, leaving an opening as shown in the diagram. It's better to leave the gap in the seam rather than at the point end as it will be much easier to sew up at the end.

3. Turn the body so the right sides are outside and mark the centre point with a thread or glass-headed pin.

4. Insert the inner head through the opening and place it at the centre point, inside the body. Gather the body fabric around the head, adjusting the fabric so there are as few creases as possible at one side, (this will be the front). Wrap strong thread around the neck several times and then fasten in place with a knot. The loose ends of the knot can either be trimmed or, for extra strength, sewn down at the neck.

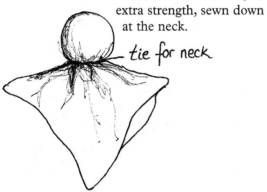

tie for neck

5. Close the gap in the seam by sewing together with a few small stitches. Tie an overhand knot at each of the top corners to represent hands.

Hat
1. Fold the hat fabric into a rectangle 10″ x 4″ (25cm x 10cm) and cut as shown in the diagram.

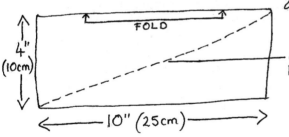

FOLD

4″
(10cm)

cut
here

10″ (25cm)

2. With the right sides of the material together, sew the back seam of the hat.

3. **Bell** (*optional*)
A small bell can be sewn inside the hat at this point.

Sew it to the seam allowance 4″ (10cm) from the pointy end.

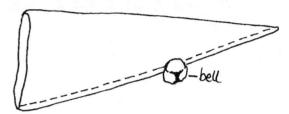

—bell

4. Turn the hat so the right side of the material is to the outside and put on the doll's head. Turn the raw edge at the bottom of the hat to the inside so it can't be seen. Sew the hat to the head, making sure all the raw edges are hidden.

5. Tie an overhand knot at the top of the hat.

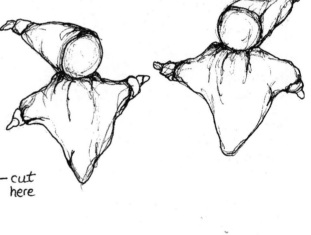

Chapter 1

General Techniques

It is worth taking the time to read through this chapter and also all the instructions for your chosen doll before starting to work, so that you understand what is involved and check on your knowledge of the techniques necessary for the whole project.

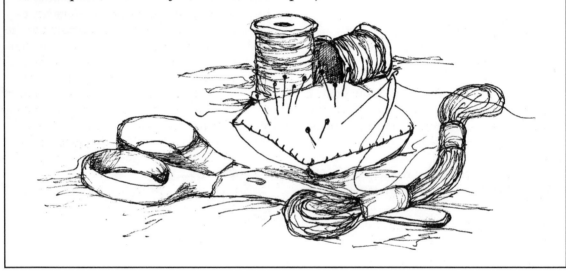

Safety

Safety is mostly a matter of common sense, making sure there are no potentially dangerous items such as buttons, beads etc. or parts which can be pulled off and swallowed by a young child or baby. The type of yarn and style of hair must be carefully considered when making a doll for a baby or toddler– it should not have bits of fluff or fibre which can be picked off and put in the mouth.

General Sewing Equipment

You will need all the ordinary items as used for dressmaking – sewing machine (but see note later), sewing thread, sharp scissors (large and small), tape measure, thimble etc.

Pins

Large glass- or plastic-headed pins are best to use as they are easier to see and less likely to get left in the doll accidentally. If you are using ordinary pins then count out a small number, perhaps 10 or 20, use only these and check you have the correct number when the project is finished.

Three glass-headed pins are essential for marking the position of the eyes and mouth.

Old scissors

Keep a pair of old scissors for cutting out the paper patterns; using your good scissors for paper and card will make them blunt.

Embroidery cotton/floss

This comes in small six-stranded skeins and is available in many colours. It is used for the eyes and mouth. All six strands are needed for marking the features on medium to large dolls, fewer on the small dolls.

It is possible to mix threads to obtain a particular eye colour. For example you could use two strands of brown, two dark green and two turquoise to get a hazel coloured eye.

Various shades of pink, red or coral floss are available for lips. Coral gives a very natural look, especially with darker hair, and provides a good contrast to brown eyes.

Think about the balance between eye, mouth and hair colours. The tonal quality of the three should be similar: bright blue eyes and scarlet lips with very pale blond hair would put undue emphasis on the features, whereas very pale features with strong red hair would mean the face would fade into insignificance. The aim is to achieve a balance of colour so all three – eyes, mouth and hair – are equally pleasing. Embroidery thread can also be used instead of knitting yarn for hair on small sized dolls.

Strong thread

Used for tying off and shaping the inner head and also to keep the skin coverings in place before assembling the doll.

Any thin strong thread can be used – I use crochet cotton (3 or 4 ply or sports weight). It must be mercerised – with a firm twist – so it does not break easily. Thin cotton string, button hole or linen thread can also be used. The thread should not be so thin that it cuts into your fingers as you pull and knot it.

Double sewing cotton or thin crochet thread (as used for lace making) is used for the small dolls.

Stuffing

The best stuffing for these dolls is sheep's wool. This natural fibre is soft, springy and amazingly good to touch. Natural fibres are also ecological: they are sustainable and re-useable.

You may be fortunate enough to be able to buy fleece in a ready-to-use state (see Suppliers) in which case just tear off pieces and use as you need. Otherwise you will have to buy fleece as it comes from the sheep and launder it. This is a very simple process which your children will enjoy helping with. Small quantities of sheepswool can often be found on hedges or fences while on country walks. It is advisable to ask permission from the farmer before taking the wool; you may even find he has a fleece tucked away in a barn which can be bought at a reasonable price. Fleece can often be bought directly from the farmer during the sheep shearing season, in England this is early summer(May or June) – try looking in your local business phone book under 'Farmers'.

Choosing fleece

The best type of fleece to use for stuffing is one with a short staple (fibre length) and medium softness. Speciality fleece from sheep such as Jacob's is wonderful for spinners but too soft for stuffing dolls. Dark coloured wool may well show through the lighter shades of skin fabric, also where the fleece is not a uniform colour (some fleece have patches of grey, brown and white) this may well give the finished doll a blotchy appearance. The solution is either to pre-sort the fleece before using or to use a double layer of fabric for the doll.

Washing fleece

Unwashed fleece can be a little smelly and is full of lanolin, so protect your clothes with an apron or overall.

A whole fleece weighs 3 - 5lb (1.5 - 2.5kg) and is sufficient for several dolls – maybe you could share a fleece with a friend.

First unroll the fleece, preferably outside, and break off any very muddy or dirty bits around the edges. These can go in the compost bucket. Now pull off about a third of the fleece to wash. Store the rest in a closed bag in a dry place.

Put the selected wool in a bucket or bowl of warm water and soak for 1 - 2 hours. Lift the fleece out of the bucket, leaving most of the mud and dirt behind. This stage can be omitted if your fleece is relatively clean.

Fill a clean bowl with warm water and dissolve a cup of detergent and add the fleece. It is important to use detergent, rather than soap flakes or a wool wash, because this helps to remove the grease in the wool which otherwise might later come through the skin fabric and leave dirty marks on the doll.

Wash the fleece by gently moving it around in the water to release the dirt and grease. Remove the wool from the water and repeat the washing process if necessary.

Rinse the fleece in plenty of warm water, and squeeze out excess moisture. Felting or matting of the wool occurs if the water used is too hot or the fleece is handled too roughly. Treat it like an expensive wool sweater.

Dry the wool by laying it on towels or other absorbent cloths in a warm room, turning over as necessary.

If your washing machine has a spin only facility then use this to remove excess moisture. Put the fleece in a pillowcase and tie up the top before spinning. Spread out on a towel and dry as described above.

Preparing the fleece before use
Once the fleece is clean it must be carded or teased, the aim being to separate the fibres and remove any odd bits of dust or twig that remain.

Carders are pieces of wood with handles that have a mat of strong wires protruding. These wires have hooks or barbs which catch the wool and pull the fibres (or staple) into parallel lines. Carders are used by spinners and felt makers and are obtainable wherever supplies for these crafts are sold.

Put a small quantity of wool on one carder and hold the handle firmly with one hand. Grasp the second carder in the other hand, and wire mesh facing, pull across the surface of the first. Fleece will transfer from one carder to the other.

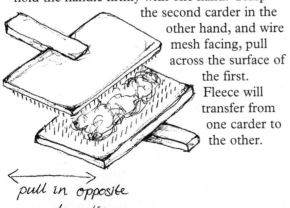

pull in opposite directions

Continue until the fibres of the fleece are lying parallel to each other and to the short sides of the carder. It is important to work in the same direction each time (from top to bottom). Remove the fleece by pulling it gently from the bottom of the carder. Repeat this process until you have a large pile of stuffing ready to use.

Teasing
If you do not have carders then the fleece can be teased. Pull off a handful of fleece and break it into small bits with your fingers, discarding any dust or twigs. The aim is to separate the wool into its strands or fibres which will make a pile of soft fluffy wool for stuffing.

Quantities – a guide
Sheepswool is a natural fibre and does not come in standardised bundles, it can vary in texture, fibre length and density not only from one fleece to another but also from one part of the fleece to another. I have given the weight of wool needed with individual instructions but this can only be a guide. Other measurements, such as the circumference of an inner head, are given to help with this problem but ultimately you, as the creator of the doll, have to decide on the correct quantities.

Alternatives
Kapok – a natural vegetable fibre. It is very dense, cannot be washed and is messy to work with. It gives satisfactory results for heads made from tubular cotton.

Shredded knitting yarn – either use left over balls of wool or recycle from old knitted garments. Only satisfactory for very small projects as it becomes lumpy over larger areas. If the yarn is brightly coloured it will show through light coloured fabric.

Lentils or rice: can be used for bodies of fabric dolls (i.e. not under cotton knit or skin fabric) but gives a very different feel and cannot be washed.

Polyester – washable and easily obtainable, can be used where there is an allergy to wool. It is very soft in use and at the same time unyielding – the dolls may look similar but will feel very different.

Not recommended, but if you do use it then buy the best quality as it has more 'loft' or springiness. This stuffing gives bulk but little weight, giving a deceptive feel to the doll for a child.

Dolls with fabric bodies (e.g. velour or brushed cotton) need less stuffing but you should be able to squeeze quite hard and not feel the back and front body fabric rubbing together.

Stuffing – tools and techniques
Stuffing sticks – any thin blunt stick can be used to help with stuffing: dowel in various thickness, blunt pencils, knob end of knitting needle etc.

Tweezers – useful for stuffing the very smallest dolls, to push wool into tiny legs and arms.

Stuffing dolls is definitely an art, it takes care and practice to get a smooth, firm and resilient body that keeps its intended shape.

The most important thing is to use small pieces of fluffy sheep's wool and to make sure no gaps are left between one piece of stuffing and the next. Lumpy dolls are the result of uneven stuffing which has not filled all the space available.

When stuffing narrow pieces, such as legs, push a ball of wool right down to the toes using a stuffing tool as necessary. Reshape the leg after each piece of stuffing is put in place to avoid the fabric stretching too much. Expect to use more stuffing than you first thought necessary. It should be packed down well so that the doll keeps its shape even after much wear and washing.

Knitting yarn
Used for hair and for making clothes.

Pure wool usually in double knit or 4 ply weights (worsted and sports weight) – best for durability and obtainable in lots of colours.

Textured yarns – mohair, bouclé, slubs etc. Chose yarn with high wool content.

Cotton yarn – looks good but does not wear as well as wool. Best for smaller dolls.

Novelty yarns – some of which contain silk, kid mohair or cashmere – feel beautiful but are very soft and may break or pull easily. Use them in combination with other more sturdy yarns, or for knitted or crocheted hair styles.

Specialist needles
Doll-making needle – this is a long, thin but strong needle used for sewing the features on the face. It needs to be at least 4 - 5″ (10 - 12cm) long and is often labelled as a 'long darner'. Needles sold for upholstery are longer but usually too thick; they leave unsightly holes in the cotton skin fabric.

Embroidery needles – a medium length needle with a large eye and sharp point is needed for embroidered hair and is useful for sewing the strings on the inner heads. These needles are sold for embroidery or crewelwork. Tapestry needles are too blunt and therefore not suitable.

Fabrics
Skin fabric – cotton knit or stockinette is used for all the dolls in this book. It is a knitted fabric and has clear ribs running down. The fabric stretches both ways but is most elastic across the ribs. The amount of stretch varies according to the type and sometimes even colour of the fabric. My patterns are based on a medium stretch – 2″ (5cm) of fabric will stretch to 4″ (10cm) when pulled to its maximum. Fold the material over and do this test at least 2″ (5cm) away from the cut edge of the fabric, as it will

STRETCH GUIDE

4″ (10 cm)

2″ (5cm)
FABRIC

WILL STRETCH TO HERE

stretch more at the edge. If your fabric stretch is greatly different then you will need to adjust the patterns to compensate for this, increasing or decreasing the width of bodies, limbs etc.

This fabric is most commonly available in a cream or flesh colour, but other colours suitable for ethnic dolls can sometimes be bought. You may have to use brown T-shirts, new or recycled, or dye white fabric to get the shade you want. Always wash these dark materials before use in case there is excessive dye left in the fabric.

Velour – cotton velour has a beautiful soft touch which just demands to be hugged. It comes in many colours and is perfect for soft dolls. Make sure the percentage of cotton is high (75% or more) as synthetic velour is not nearly so appealing.

Velour has a pile – there is a clear direction to the fabric. Stroke it with your hand and you will feel it is smoother one way than the other. All the pattern pieces must be cut with the pile or nap going the same way. There is difference in colour, depending on the direction of the pile, more noticeable in some shades than others.

Cotton fabric - various woven cotton fabrics are suitable for soft doll bodies: brushed cotton, winceyette and flannelette, as used for nightwear, are soft and cuddly while corduroy or needlecord makes a sturdy body. Plain cotton can be good too.

The faces and hands of sack dolls can be made from skin-coloured velour or from closely knit wool jumpers. This is an especially good solution for ethnic dolls where there may be a problem in getting the correct colour for the skin.

I do not recommend making an entire limb doll from these materials. They do not hold the stuffing satisfactorily and soon sag and become shapeless. A partial solution to this problem is to line the outer skin fabric with a thin cotton knit – lay the two fabrics together and sew as if they are one. It is not easy to work in this way and is suggested for experienced sewers only.

A wool garment that has been washed at too

high a temperature and has felted makes a good firm fabric for faces. Dolls made from these fabrics need little or no added hair; they are complete in themselves.

Paints, pencils and crayons

Artist-quality coloured pencils can be used for eyes, freckles etc. The colour will fade with time but can easily be renewed.

Apply red beeswax crayon or rouge to the cheeks to give a healthy glow to the face.

Fabric paint can also be used but with care: the colours are harsh when used straight from the bottle, so always practise on a scrap of fabric first.

Whenever you draw or paint on a doll's face do it out of sight of your children or they may be tempted to copy you.

Re-cycled materials

T-shirts – good for making the inner head of the doll. The T-shirt needs to be a lighter colour than the skin fabric. A good quality T-shirt can be used for skin fabric – but do check the stretch against the guide given above.

Velour clothing – excellent for soft dolls, pouch or sack dolls. Often the variety of colours and quality are superior to material bought from a fabric shop.

Used clothes – corduroy, brushed cotton, stretch towelling and other suitable materials can be re-cycled from good quality used clothing. Use children's out-grown garments to make dolls' clothing – with imaginative pattern placement you can save a lot of work by re-using buttonholes, hems and collars. It is good to use a favourite item of clothing which is outgrown

but still well-loved and can help to form an immediate bond between the doll and owner.

Knitted clothes – soft lambswool and angora machine knitted clothes can be re-cycled to make bodies for sack dolls. These are wonderfully soft and perfect for a night-time cuddly doll. Try to position the pattern pieces to make the best use of the ribs (e.g. around the face edge of a hat) and machine zigzag or oversew around the raw edges of each piece as soon as it is cut, to prevent fraying.

Hand knitted garments – (when the colour is suitable) can be unpicked and used for curly hair.

Tubular stockinette

The original use for this material is as medical bandage and so is generally available in a pharmacy or chemist shop rather than a craft store. It comes in various widths and thickness. Finger bandage or gauze tubing is a fine tube made from a mix of cotton and viscose and is sold in widths of $1/2''$ or $3/4''$ (12 or 18mm). I use this for small heads.

Thicker cotton tubing of $2''$ (5cm) wide is used to form the inner head and body of the sack doll.

Rectangles of cotton knit or re-cycled T-shirts can be sewn together to make a substitute for tubular bandage.

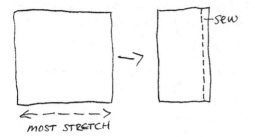

MOST STRETCH

The amount of stretch will vary according to the fabric used, so check the measurements after stuffing. Make sure the seam of your tube falls at the back of the doll's head when you tie off the inner head.

Patterns

All the pattern pieces given in this book are full size and have **no seam allowances** included, unless otherwise stated. Use thin white paper and trace off the pieces needed. Cut out the shapes and lay these on your chosen fabric, taking note where two thicknesses and/or folds of fabric are indicated. The grain line is shown on all patterns. This line should be parallel (equal distance) to the selvedge (woven edge) on woven fabric or parallel to the ribs on knit fabric.

Draw round the patterns with tailor's chalk, lead pencil or (very lightly) ballpoint pen. Cut out the pieces $1/2''$ (1cm) outside this line to give a seam allowance. This method allows you to mark an accurate line to sew on.

For very small or intricate pieces it is easier to draw round the pattern, stitch round the shape and then cut out close to the seam.

Pattern symbols

The following pattern symbols are used throughout the book:

Grain line – Place this line parallel to the selvedge (finished edge of the fabric) or parallel to the rib on knitted fabric.

Most stretch (knit fabrics only) – place the pattern with the most stretch of the fabric (across the rib) as indicated by the arrow.

Fold – place the pattern on the fold of the fabric.

CF

Centre front – marks the centre of the front of the pattern piece.

CB

Centre back – marks the centre of the back of the pattern piece.

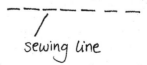

sewing line

Sewing line – the actual line on which the seam is made.

Sewing techniques
Sewing machine

It is easier and quicker to sew the main seams on a machine.

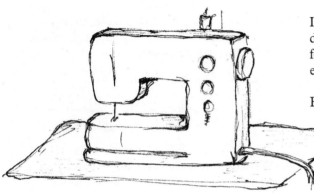

Some machines may have problems sewing cotton knit fabric. You will have to experiment with scraps of fabric to get your tension and stitch length right.

I use a ballpoint needle in my machine. This is specially made for knit fabrics and will slip between the knitted rows in the fabric rather than piercing the material and perhaps causing a ladder or hole. Sewing machine needles need to be changed frequently, a blunt needle is often the cause of skipped stitches, pulling threads or uneven tension.

The seam must stretch slightly when sewing cotton knit or it will break if it comes under stress (usually as you stuff the doll). I find using a fairly small stitch length and a slight zigzag work best on my machine. I also loosen the tension a little. Check by pulling on a seam made in scrap fabric; it should give slightly and not snap the threads in the seam.

Velour, corduroy and other fabrics do not usually give any problem when sewn on the machine.

Hand sewing

When starting and finishing never use a knot, this makes a weak point which will eventually break through. Instead take two or more tiny stitches at the same point to hold the thread securely.

I like to hide the ends of my thread inside the doll. This is especially important when sewing features with embroidery thread otherwise the ends always seem to poke out through the hair.

Begin by pushing the threaded needle in some distance from your intended starting place. Bring it up at the correct place (B) and pull the end of the thread through the fabric until it just disappears inside the doll (A). Take two small stitches to secure the thread.

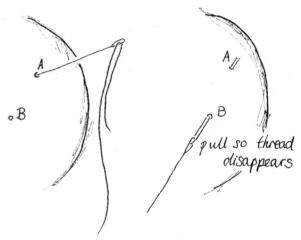

When ending, bring your needle to the desired place, take two small stitches and then push the needle and thread through the fabric 2″ (5cm) from your finishing place, pull the thread taut and snip close to the fabric. The end should disappear inside.

Stitches used

Running stitch – used for gathers. Take the needle in and out of the fabric at regularly spaced intervals. The thread can be pulled up to gather the fabric.

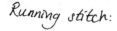

Use this stitch to sew down yarn for hair and also at neck, wrists and ankles of soft dolls.

In this case the raw edge of the fabric is turned to the inside and the running stitch is made through two thicknesses.

Backstitch – used to join two pieces of fabric together. The individual stitches need to be small or pieces of stuffing will come through. It

can be used whenever instructions say to machine a seam.

Catch stitch – a hemming or invisible stitch. It is used mostly to join heads to bodies or arms

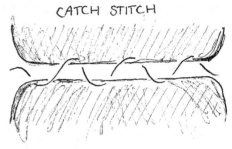

to hands as neatly as possible. It involves taking tiny running stitches first at one side and then the other.

Stab stitch – used to form lines for leg joints on traditional dolls. Put the threaded needle through all thicknesses of the fabric to the back, pull the thread through and then bring the needle and thread back to the right side a short way along. This looks like running stitch

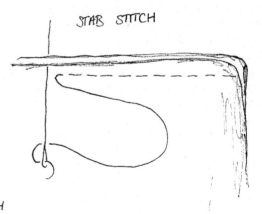

but the needle should always be held vertically (at 90 degrees) to the fabric – thus giving a strong accurate stitch.

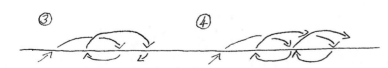

French knot – a decorative stitch used to supplement embroidered hair. Thread needle with a length of yarn. Take a short stitch to start and then make another stitch but do not pull the needle all the way through. Wind the yarn round the sharp end of the needle three times. Pull yarn through these loops. Take a stitch to secure the knot and finish off.

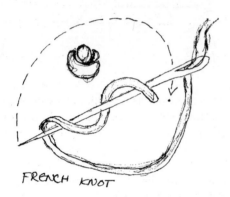

FRENCH KNOT

Caring for your dolls

With a little care and attention these handmade dolls will last for many years. It is a good idea to set aside a time at least once a year, perhaps during the summer holidays, to examine your dolls and repair as necessary. Small holes can be mended, hair resewn and doll and clothes washed ready for the next year. For one family I know this annual renovation is timed to coincide with a visit from their grandparents and new clothes are also made. Each doll has to have a new item of clothing – even if it's just a waistcoat (vest) or ribbons for their hair and the whole process becomes a family affair.

When more extensive repairs become necessary most parts of the doll can be renovated and renewed. Patch large holes in the skin fabric by using the original pattern to cut out new pieces. Hand sew in place on top of the original. If the hair becomes thin then add an extra layer or two on top of the existing wool. It is also possible to remove the original hair and sew a completely new hairstyle onto the doll. Extra stuffing can be added by making an opening in an unobtrusive place, putting carded fleece inside and sewing up.

Do consult the owner of the doll before making any major repairs; he or she may not see the alterations in quite the same way as an adult. The blemishes and worn patches have become an integral part of the character of the doll and the child may strongly resist any changes.

Washing instructions

All the dolls from this book, except the small doll containing pipecleaners, can be washed by hand. Dissolve a small amount of soap powder or proprietary wool wash in a bowl of warm water and gently wash the doll. Rinse well in lots of clean water, squeeze to remove excess water and reshape the doll. Wrap in a towel and hang up to dry.

Small areas, such as hands and face, can be cleaned by rubbing with an almost dry bar of soap and then with a damp flannel.

Chapter 2

Hair

Sewing the hair is the final and perhaps the most creative part of making the doll. The possibilities are endless. Remember that people have all sorts of different textures and colours in their hair so reflect this in your doll.

Safety

Whatever hairstyle you choose make sure all the strands of wool are securely sewn in and cannot easily be pulled out. Fluffy yarns like mohair or bouclé can be shredded and perhaps swallowed by a very young child. If there is likely to be a problem then sew on a little bonnet or scarf to cover the head, which can be removed in a year or so. Another solution is to plait or braid long hair and fasten the ends so they cannot be undone.

Materials

I prefer to use natural yarns wherever possible, pure wool is the most versatile and lasts well. Cotton can look good, especially for Asian hair, but may eventually break or unravel. Mohair with just a small percentage of nylon gives a beautifully bouncy effect like newly washed human hair – it will flatten after repeated washing so always use it together with other yarns.

I like to use a mixture of colours, weights and textures when making dolls' hair as I feel this gives a more interesting and realistic effect. My 'standard' mix would be one strand of mohair and two strands of medium weight wool (double knit) each in different but toning colours.

Occasionally I use as many as six or seven different yarns – especially if I want to put hair on an ethnic doll where the hair colour is perceived as black. Here I use one strand of black mohair, one strand brown mohair plus four or five shades of brown, black and auburn. This gives a much better effect than using black alone.

I use thick yarn (chunky or aran) for short hair – especially for boy dolls.

Basic long hair: sewn on

Materials: for dolls up to 20" (45cm) tall
1oz (25gm) mohair
2oz (50gm) pure wool
(double knit or medium weight) in desired colours
matching sewing cotton

Method

1. Measure doll from top of head to top of legs (or wherever hair has to finish). Double this measurement and add on 1″ (2.5cm) to work out the length you need.

For example, where the finished length = 12″ (30cm) then

$$12 \times 2 = 24$$
$$24 + 1 = 25 \text{ inches}$$

or

$$30 \times 2 = 60$$
$$60 + 2.5 = 62.5\text{cm}$$

So you need a total length of 25″ (62.5cm) for each piece of yarn.

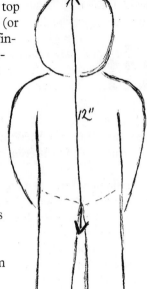

12″

Using all 3 strands of yarn together (1 mohair and 2 wool) measure out pieces of wool 25″ (62.5cm) in length. There need to be sufficient strands to cover the doll's head from the front hairline to the crown of the head.

2. Put a glass-headed pin at the centre front of the doll's head where the parting will begin. Put another pin directly behind this at the crown of the head (just before it begins to slope inwards to the neck). Arrange the cut lengths of yarn between these two pins. They should form a thin, but even layer with the skin fabric completely covered. Adjust as necessary by adding or taking away the yarn.

When you have arranged the hair neatly then tie around the neck with a ribbon or tape to hold in place while you sew.

3. Thread a sewing needle with cotton to match the hair colour and sew the yarn to the head with small running stitches. It is easier to sew from back to front two or three times than to try to catch every piece of wool with one row of stitches.

4. Pull the hair at the back of the head so that it meets, retie ribbon at neck if necessary. Now sew around the hair from one side to the other. The first line is about 2″ (5cm) from the centre

centre parting

— 1st line

— 2nd line

parting and the second starts at the eye line and dips slightly at the back following the contours of the head. The head should be covered with wool with no skin fabric peeping through. Remove the pins.

5. Put two more layers of hair on top of this first one. Measure, cut and arrange the second layer as you did before. Make sure that the hair meets at the centre back – adding extra lengths of wool as necessary.

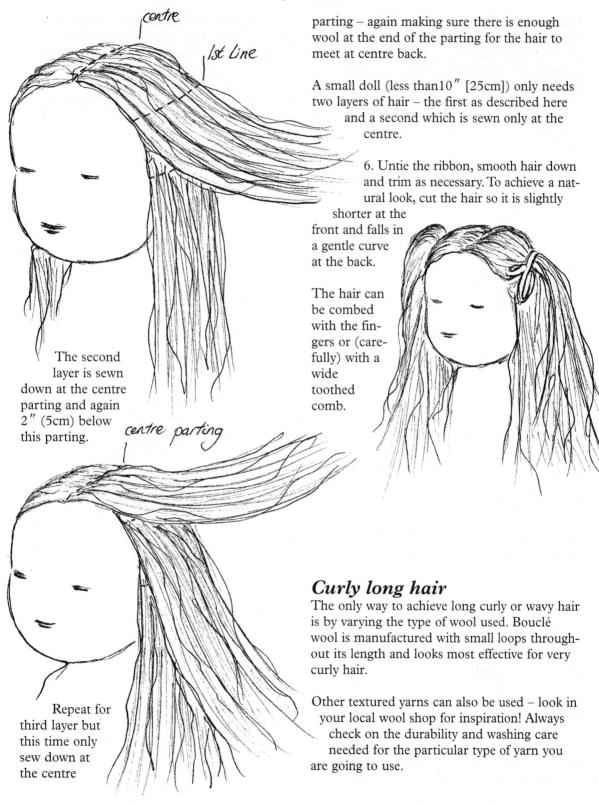

centre

1st Line

parting – again making sure there is enough wool at the end of the parting for the hair to meet at centre back.

A small doll (less than 10″ [25cm]) only needs two layers of hair – the first as described here and a second which is sewn only at the centre.

6. Untie the ribbon, smooth hair down and trim as necessary. To achieve a natural look, cut the hair so it is slightly shorter at the front and falls in a gentle curve at the back.

The hair can be combed with the fingers or (carefully) with a wide toothed comb.

The second layer is sewn down at the centre parting and again 2″ (5cm) below this parting.

centre parting

Repeat for third layer but this time only sew down at the centre

Curly long hair

The only way to achieve long curly or wavy hair is by varying the type of wool used. Bouclé wool is manufactured with small loops throughout its length and looks most effective for very curly hair.

Other textured yarns can also be used – look in your local wool shop for inspiration! Always check on the durability and washing care needed for the particular type of yarn you are going to use.

Follow the instructions for basic long hair, but use bouclé or other textured yarn – perhaps mixed with other wools, in place of the recommended wool and mohair.

Pre-knitted yarn can also be used for an extra curly look. Recycle an existing jumper by

bouclé wool

pre knitted yarns

unpicking the yarn and sewing it to the doll's head; or knit up new yarn, dampen and dry before unravelling. When the doll is washed the curl will drop out a little but can be revitalised by dampening and winding round rags, pipe cleaners or covered wire. Fasten securely and leave for a day or two while the hair dries. Undo to reveal lots of curls.

Variations

Fringe or bangs

These look most natural when applied as an extra layer at the beginning of the process described above.

Method

1. Measure from the eyes over head to top of legs at the centre back (or length desired). Add 1″ (2.5cm) for trimming and styling the hair.

2. Use this measurement to cut strands of your yarn (one mohair plus two wool). You need enough to lay flat across the doll's head and reach from one eye to the other.

3. Sew, using matching thread, with small running stitches across the top of the fringe where the natural hair line would be.

4. Sew another line of stitches parallel to the first row but about 2″ (5cm) further back.

Now continue as for the basic long hair starting at #1 and putting the next three layers over this one. There is no need to pull the first layer of hair to meet at the back (see #4) because there is wool already in place – just sew it down with the hair at the side. The wool must meet at the back on the second and third layers to give an even hair style.

When you have finished, trim the hair at the front so the eyes can be seen but do not cut it too short or the fringe will stick up at the front.

Short hair

Measure and cut lengths of wool so that the final length reaches to the shoulders. Short hair styles look more natural and better balanced with a fringe.

Trim the hair to give the desired style. Each layer can be cut slightly shorter than the previous one to give a shaped look. Short hair is often most effective either with several thin yarns or just one chunky. Omitting the mohair gives a sleeker look which is appropriate for an older boy's hair style.

Sewing from the crown

Many young children have a cap of hair cut to fall from the crown of their head without a parting and this style tries to capture that look. It is only suitable for short hair.

Method

1. Mark the crown or centre point of the head with a glass-headed pin.

2. Start at the back of the head and measure from the pin to the shoulder. Double this measurement and add 1″ (2.5cm). Using your chosen yarn or mixture of yarns cut ten to twelve pieces of wool to this length.

3. Fold cut lengths of yarn in half and, sewing through all the strands at the centre, attach to the crown as marked by the pin.

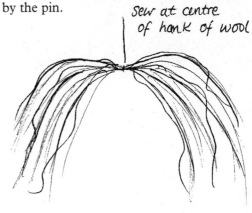

Sew at centre of hank of wool

4. Repeat this process all round the head.

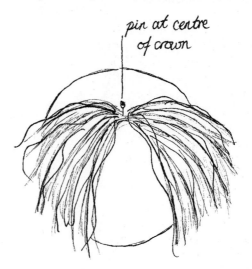

pin at centre of crown

You will need to remeasure each hank or group of yarn pieces, as the length will vary as you move around the head. Spread out the yarn as you go so that all the skin fabric is covered.

5. Sew around the circumference of the head 1½ - 2″ (4 - 5cm) from the centre point. Sew with matching thread and use small running stitches – go round twice to make sure all the yarn is sewn to the head.

6. Sew another line of stitches below the first.

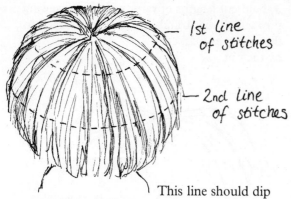

1st line of stitches

2nd line of stitches

This line should dip at the back to represent a natural hair line. Again make sure all the pieces of yarn are sewn securely to the head. Remove the pin.

7. Repeat this process from #2 with two more layers for a large doll (over 12″ [30cm]) but only one for a smaller doll.

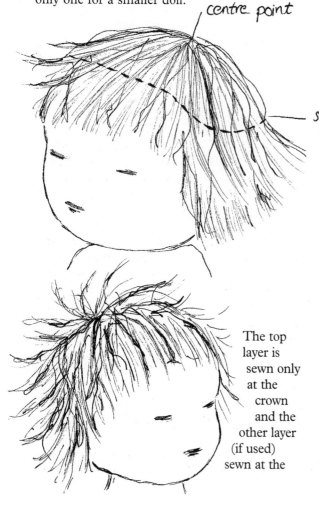

centre point

stitching line

The top layer is sewn only at the crown and the other layer (if used) sewn at the

crown and 1 - 2″ (3 - 5cm) from the centre point. Trim as necessary.

Embroidered hair

Embroidered or sewn hair looks very attractive and is much safer for a small child as there are no loose ends to chew or choke on. This type of hair style will stay neater and cleaner for a longer time than sewn on styles, and as such would be more suitable for a doll used at playgroup or kindergarten.

The main disadvantage is that it cannot be easily changed, braided or played with and does not look as natural as long flowing tresses. It is also quite time-consuming to apply as each strand has to be sewn in place individually. I have devised one method which is quicker to make but still has the appearance and most of the advantages of sewn on hair.

Materials
All these styles need only small amounts of yarn: one ball (25gm) of mohair and one (50gm) of wool will be ample for any of the following styles

Wrap and sew
This method gives a smooth cap of hair starting from a centre point on top of the head.

Materials
Yarn in desired colour – wool or wool and mohair
Sewing thread to match
Two sewing needles
Glass-headed pins

Method
1. Thread both needles with doubled sewing thread in a colour to match the hair wool. Take

one needle and make several small stitches at the centre or crown of the head (just before it begins to slope back to the neck). When the thread is firmly attached to the head stick about half the needle into the head itself leaving the eye end sticking out.

2. Place the glass-headed pins all the way around the head on the hair line (i.e. where you want the hair to finish). The pins should be about 1/4″ (0.5cm) apart.

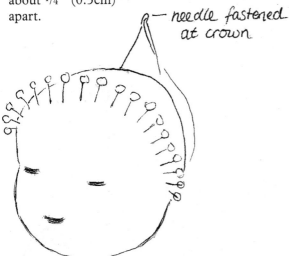

needle fastened at crown

3. Take two strands of your chosen yarn (one mohair and one wool or two of wool) and use the needle and thread at the crown to hold them in place. Do this by taking one or two small stitches right through the yarn about 1″ (2.5cm) from its end. Replace needle in its upright position.

4. Wind the two strands of yarn from the centre to a pin at the back of the head, around this pin and back around the centre needle. Repeat this around six to eight consecutive pins or until the needle has yarn about halfway up its protruding length.

Pull the needle out of the head, its thread should come through the yarn loops you have just made. Sew these down at the crown with one or two stitches and replace the needle in its original position.

5. With the other threaded needle sew the loops at the hair line in place. Start the thread with two small stitches on the head, near the first pin you have used. Remove the first pin and

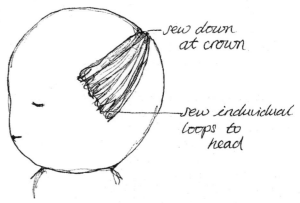

sew down at crown

sew individual loops to head

sew down the loop of wool. Do the same with each loop, removing the pins as you go.

6. Repeat this process right around the head. You may need to alter the spacing of the pins, depending on the thickness of the yarn you are using. The idea is to make a close fitting cap of hair with no skin fabric showing.

7. When you have covered the entire head cut the yarn, leaving 2″ (5cm) after the last loop has been made. Tuck this inside the hair next to the scalp and sew down with a couple of little stitches. Fasten the sewing thread at the centre of the head and at the face edge with a few small stitches hidden under the hair wool.

Variations
Pony tail
Add a pony tail which can have pretty ribbon tied around or be put in braids for added fun.

Cut pieces of yarn twice the desired length of the pony tail. Fold in half and sew the centre of

the yarn lengths to the crown of the head. Take several stitches, with matching sewing thread, right through the bundle of yarn so it is held very securely. Fasten off. Trim pony tail as desired.

Braids or bunches
This variation is more difficult to achieve because the pins have to be placed very neatly at the centre parting if a realistic effect is to result.

1. The hair is sewn on one half of the head at a time. Put a line of pins straight down the head to form a centre parting and put the needle at the side, at the place where the braid or bunch is to start.

side view of pins

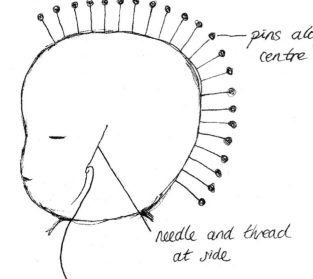

pins along centre parting

needle and thread at side

2. Wind the hair round from the needle to the pin and back to the needle as described previously. Repeat for the other side of the head.

3. Cut pieces of yarn twice the desired length of the loose hair and sew the centre of this yarn to the side of the head at the appropriate place. Trim.

side view with braid added

Embroidered hair

In its simplest form this means just sewing a thread across the head from a centre point to the hair line and repeating this until the scalp is covered. It takes practice and some skill to achieve a smooth and even hair style.

Sewing needle – choose your needle with care; it needs to be sturdy but not so thick it will make a hole in the fabric and needs a eye large enough to thread with knitting wool. Needles sold for darning should meet these requirements. It is worth spending time to find a good needle as this will make the job much easier and quicker.

Start with a small doll, 10″ - 12″ (25cm - 30cm) at most, and use short lengths of wool

(20″/50cm) which are not too thick. Pulling the yarn through the fabric can lead to splitting and breaking if the yarn is too long. Yarn sold for embroidery is stronger but expensive to buy in large quantities.

If you are able to obtain weaving yarn this is a good alternative; it is very strong but is thin and so a great many stitches would be needed.

Method

1. Mark the hair line – that is where you want the hair to end on the doll. You can make a faint pencil line or put pins in at intervals. Check it is even and follows the contours of the head.

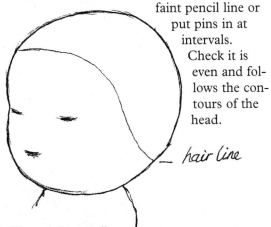

hair line

2. Thread the needle with a length of yarn. If the yarn is very thin then use a double thread. Start near the hair line with a small stitch or a French knot (see chapter on **General Techniques**). Take a stitch from the hair line to the centre pulling the yarn so it lies snugly across the head.

Take a small stitch at the top of the head and then another stitch to the hair line. Repeat until the whole head is covered. Add extra short stitches from the hairline part way to the crown in order to cover the head without lumps or gaps.

3. Larger heads – these need rows of shorter parallel stitches. Mark the hair line as before and then, starting at the crown, take long stitches of varying length (2 - 3″ [5 - 8cm]) radiating out from the centre.

Add a second row below this of straight stitches parallel to each other and staggered so that all the head is covered with stitches. Further rows may be needed depending on the size of the head.

4. Check the hair for gaps and lumps – fill these in with extra stitches or a cluster of French knots. Extra pieces of yarn can be sewn on for a wispy or baby style.

Variations

It is possible to add pony tails and braids as described for the *Wrap and sew* hair styles.

Shaggy hair

A doll with this hair style is probably the most endearing of all. Unfortunately a mophead is also the most time-consuming of all the styles and must be made with strong but thin yarn to get the best results. Weaving or Scandinavian Rya type wool is ideal – otherwise try a tightly spun three or four ply (sports weight).

Method

1. Cover the head with one layer of the chosen yarn as described for hair sewn from the crown. The finished length of this layer should reach to the shoulders.

2. Thread a needle with one or two strands of yarn (depending on thickness of yarn). Start at

loops of yarn

the hair line and work a row of rug stitches (Turkish knot stitches) right round the head.

3. Insert needle into fabric leaving a short end hanging free. Hold this down with the thumb (a). Bring the needle up close to this hanging thread and take a stitch to the right (b). Bring the needle up just to the left of this loop (c) and leave a loop of yarn before starting on the next stitch. Note the start and finish of the stitch is between the same two threads of the upper horizontal stitch.

Continue working this stitch round and round the head until it is completely covered (follow numbers 1-5 on the diagram).

loose end

loop

The finished head will be a mass of loops – these can be left or cut to give a shaggy look. A gentle steaming (don't hold the head too close to the source) will enhance the fluffy effect and can revitalise a flattened hair style.

Crocheted and knitted hair

These instructions are quite general because they have to be adapted to the individual doll's head. A wig or hat is made and then sewn onto the doll's head. Compare your work with the doll as you go and remember that knitted or crocheted work is stretchy and so an exact fit is not too important.

Materials
Knitting wool or cotton used alone or with a strand of mohair added.
Crochet hook or knitting needles in a size to give a good tension – it is better to have a loose stitch than a tight one.

Crochet
Close fitting cap
Start with four or five chain stitches joined into a ring and work successive rounds of treble or double treble stitches, increasing as necessary to fit the head. Extra short rows may be needed for the back part of the head.

This cap is then sewn onto the doll's head and makes a good representation of soft baby hair, especially if made with mohair. Lengths of yarn can be knotted into the cap to make short or long hair.

Curly hair
A similar shaped wig can be made using a loop stitch. Start with a circle of chain stitches as before. The loops are formed round the first two fingers of the left hand on the back of the work.

The density of loops is varied by working into every stitch or every second or third stitch on alternate rows.

Foundation Row (right side): Make a small circle of chain stitches. Work six or seven double crochet stitches into the circle.

First Row: Make one chain to count as the first double crochet (dc). *Insert hook into next dc, hold yarn across first and second fingers of left hand and draw out yarn to the necessary length by raising the second finger. Keep the hook to the right of the yarn over the fingers, then place the hook over the yarn lying between the second and third fingers and draw a loop through the dc. Keep the hook to the left of the yarn lying over the fingers, and taking from your ball of knitting yarn, put this yarn round the hook and draw through both loops on the hook. Remove second finger from loop. The loop stitch is now completed. Repeat from * to complete the round.

Second Round: Work a row of double crochet or trebles.

These two rows form the pattern.

I do not recommend cutting the loops formed by this stitch as the work may unravel.

Knitting

The knitted cap comprises a shaped strip of fabric which is then sewn up to make a half dome or hat shape.

The bottom of the strip which goes round the face needs to be wider than the top or centre. This is best achieved by knitting part rows.

Basic shape

Cast on the required number of stitches (16 stitches are used for this example) and work three rows in the desired stitch.

*Fourth row: Work twelve stitches, turn and work back on these twelve only.

Fifth row: Work all sixteen stitches. Work another three rows and repeat from *.

Garter or plain stitch

Work every row knit, making part rows as necessary.

Use thin wool or mohair and fine needles to give a close fuzzy look – ideal for a young child's hair.

Use two or more strands of yarn and different sized needles (one thick, one thin) to make hair for a black doll. It gives the look of rows of tiny braids. This is a good style for a doll which is to be given to a young child. The texture is pleasant for tiny fingers yet the hair cannot be easily pulled apart.

Loop stitch

Cast on an odd number of stitches.

First row (right side): Knit 1, *knit 1 without letting stitch fall from the left hand needle, bring the yarn forward and wind yarn clockwise round left thumb to make loop about 2″ (5cm) long, take the yarn back and knit into the back of the same stitch – loop stitch made – knit 1, repeat from * to end.

Second row: Knit 1, * knit 2 together, knit 1 repeat from * to end.

Third row: Knit 2, * make a loop as described for first row, knit 1, repeat from * to last stitch, knit 1.

Fourth row: Knit 2, * knit 2 together, knit 1, repeat from * to last stitch, knit 1.

This stitch can be used to make a full wig as described above or just worked as a short strip of hair for a doll which is to have a hat sewn permanently in place.

Chapter 3

Small Dolls

Small things are a mystery and delight to us all, whatever our age, so make these dolls for your children and their friends and also for yourself and your friends.

Adults are often attracted to my dolls but feel awkward about having one of their own. The little pouch dolls are ideal to give as an adult present. They can be made in strong colours or delicate Liberty type floral prints and then provided with a small bag, in matching fabric, which contains sweet-smelling pot pourri. I was once amazed to see a concert musician open her violin case to start her warm-up and then retrieve four or five little soft dolls which fell out with her instrument. After the concert she told me that they were her good luck mascots and they had travelled all over the world with her.

I made a small doll for a sick friend and added a lavender bag. She was delighted and kept her little doll under her pillow so she could smell it whenever she felt sad.

I heard another story about a dolls house doll which was given to a stroke patient, a woman called Clare. Clare was in the very early stages of recovery, and had barely regained her ability to speak. She was given a little doll dressed as an angel with a silk dress and long flowing hair. When the doll was pressed into her hand her eyes sparkled and she looked absolutely delighted with her gift. Clare struggled to find some words and finally managed to form the words 'thank you'. The little doll stayed on her bedside table and was used extensively by her speech therapist to encourage and extend vocabulary. Clare now keeps the doll on display in her living room as a reminder of those difficult times and her eventual recovery.

One family spent several Advent Sundays making a collection of the dolls with hands and feet in bright greens and reds, and then adding smart little pointed hats. They used them as decorations all over their house: on the Christmas tree, hanging from the pine branches in the hall, sitting amongst the Christmas cards and even on the wreath on the front door. Everyone who came to the house remarked on the dolls and there was a friendly competition among the visitors to see who could spot the most dolls. After Christmas the dolls were given to the local kindergarten for the children to enjoy.

The dolls described in this chapter are all less than 6″ (15cm) tall, easy to hold in the hand, quick to make, and based on the same size head. I often choose to make these small dolls when I am asked to hold workshops for groups of pre-school parents. They are a good choice to make in large numbers for a sale of work or other fundraising event and many different styles can be made by varying the colours and types of fabric.

The heads are made from narrow gauze tubing or finger bandage, which is widely available from high street chemists. The tubing used here comes in rolls ¹/₂″ (1.6cm) wide and 4¹/₂yd (4m) long, but slightly wider tubing can be used to produce the same size heads. Compare your head with the actual size drawings to ensure that it is correct. Some care is needed when stuffing because the tubing will stretch and stretch, getting fatter and shorter, unless you keep pulling it back into shape.

The pouch doll has a very simple form and makes a wonderful toy for small children and babies. It is also simple to make. An older child will be able to sew this type of doll without too much trouble. The inner head can be simplified by omitting the eyeline to give a smooth round head. Don't try to stuff the head covering alone because it is very difficult to achieve a smooth head without the inner tubing. It is best to use plain fabric in soft colours if the doll is for a young child. Stronger colours make striking dolls but are more appropriate for older children.

The angel style pouch doll can be adapted for adults. Make the doll in a fine flowered cotton, add a sweet smelling bag of pot pourri and then hang in a clothes cupboard or display in the bedroom.

The dolls house doll is a miniature version of a 'real' doll with removable clothes. She is a little more complicated to make because of the wire framework but can still be finished in a few hours. It's nice to make a whole family of these. You can enlarge the pattern a little and add a slightly bigger head to make a 6″ (15 cm) mother and father. Sew a small version of the tiny baby and put in a walnut shell cradle to complete the family group.

A different approach to covering the head, with the fabric extended to make simple hands and feet, is used for the final project described in this chapter. It is an interesting variation and very appealing.

Another use for the small head explained in this chapter is to add it to a knitted body. Simply knit, in any yarn, two pieces for the body approximately 4″ (10cm) square and sew up leaving a gap for the head. Stuff the knitted pieces and sew the head in place. Add hair or a knitted cap and use matching thread to tie off little hands and feet at each corner. Knitted in pure wool this makes a soft doll for a baby. In red or white mohair with gold stars and sequins sewn on, it becomes a special Christmas baby to display and treasure for many years.

Simple head

Materials
Finger bandage or narrow gauze tubing
Sheepswool
Cotton knit skin fabric 4″ x 4″ (10cm x 10cm)
Thin crochet cotton or string or strong sewing thread
Sewing thread to match skin fabric

Instructions

1. Cut a piece of bandage 4″ (10cm) long. Tie at one end with thin crochet cotton or strong sewing thread. Turn inside out.

2. Stuff with a small amount of carded sheepswool so that you have a sausage shape about 2″ (5cm) long. It should have sufficient stuffing to be firm but not rigid.

3. Tie at the bottom with the cotton string and tie again ¹/₂″ (1cm) from the bottom to make the neck.

— neck

Tie another piece of thick thread all the way round the head about half way between the neck and the top to make the eyeline. Pull this thread tightly so a clear indentation is made in the head.

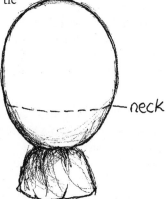

— neck Compare your head with the actual size drawing shown here.

4. Using the pattern cut out a head covering from the skin fabric.

Machine on the line shown and turn so the seam is on the inside. Put on the head with the seam at the back. Pull the fabric cover neatly over the head and tie at the neck using strong thread.

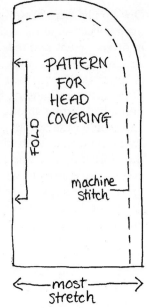

PATTERN FOR HEAD COVERING

FOLD

machine stitch

← most → stretch

5. **Face**
Using the drawing as a guide mark the position of the eyes and mouth with pins and then sew in appropriate colours. These faces are small, so sew with one strand of embroidery thread or ordinary sewing cotton.

Eyes: Start the sewing with a small stitch to hold securely at the back of the head and come through to the side of one of the pins marking the eyes; take a small straight stitch over the site of the pin. Make another stitch in exactly the same place. Repeat for the other eye and fasten off the thread at the back of the head.

Mouth: Start the thread at the back of the head again and bring the needle out a short way from the pin marking the mouth. Take one straight stitch across the pin, this should be about one and a half times the length of the eye, sew a second stitch half this size directly underneath the first. Take the thread to the back of the head and fasten off.

Alternative way to make the inner head

The method described in this section gives a more defined shape to the head. It is useful when you want a small head that is not going to have a hat sewn in place.

Follow the instructions #1 and #2 above to make the inner head.

3. Tie at the bottom with thin crochet cotton or strong thread. Tie again ¹/₂″ (1cm) from the bottom, this will be the neck.

—neck

Thread a long needle with thin crochet cotton and take two small stitches at the side of the head to fasten. Take the needle through the centre of the head to come out about half way down and then around the front half of the head to mark the eyeline. Pull on the thread so that there is a clear indentation across the face. Repeat to get another thread in the same place, then fasten with two small stitches at the side. Make a second loop starting and finishing at the same two points but this time going around the back and dipping at the centre to touch the neck. This shapes the back of the head. Finish the thread securely as before.

Compare your head with the actual size drawing shown here.

Follow instructions #4 - #7 to complete the head.

Hair
Materials
Yarn; small amounts of wool or cotton
Sewing thread to match

1. For a doll that is going to have a hat
Only the front of the hair will show and sometimes no hair at all is needed. Try the hat on and decide for yourself. If the doll is for a very young child, it is important that no bits of wool can be picked out and swallowed.

Sewn on hair: Measure across the head from one side to another (about 2″ [5cm]) and make a small hank of knitting wool this size. Place the wool at the front of the head so that the ends will be hidden by the hat. Pin the hair in place and try on hat to check the wool is in the right place and then sew firmly with matching thread at the centre and at the sides.

2. For dolls with a full head of hair
Use thin wool (3 or 4 ply) and measure sufficient to reach from one side of the head to another waist length for long hair or to the shoulder for a short style.

Thread a needle with matching sewing cotton and sew the wool down with small running stitches. Sew a line to make a centre parting and then around from one side to another at eye level. Trim to get the style you want.

Other suggestions for different hairstyles are given in the chapter on hair and these can be adapted for use with small dolls. A neat cap or just a fringe of embroidered or sewn hair is very attractive. With such a small area to work on this does not take too long.

Pouch doll

A soft squashy doll which can be made from velour, terry towelling or fine cotton. It fits snugly into a small child's hand and is easily washed.

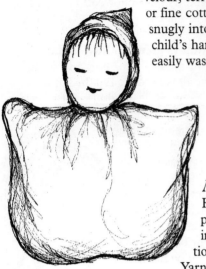

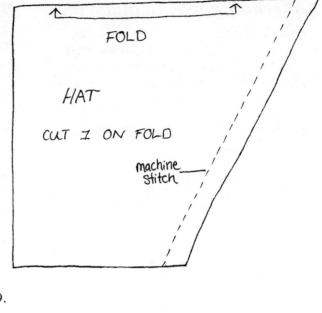

Materials
Head – see previous instructions, page 39.
Yarn for hair
10″ x 10″ (25cm x 25cm) piece of material for the body and hat
Sewing thread to match hair and body
Sheepswool 1 - 2oz (25 - 50gm)

Instructions

1. Using the actual size pattern on the right cut out a hat and body from a soft fabric – brushed cotton or velour are suitable. The material should be folded with the right sides together and the pattern placed on the folded edge of the fabric.

2. With right sides together machine or hand sew the back seam of the hat and all round the body.

3. Turn the hat so the right side of the material is outside and place on the head. Decide on the style and colour of hair, remove the hat and sew hair onto the head.

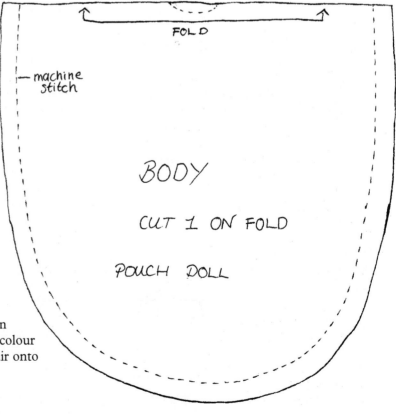

4. Replace hat on the head. Tie around the neck with sewing thread to keep in place. Using thread to match the hat fabric, sew the hat to the head with small stitches, turning in the raw edges as you go.

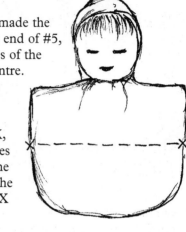

'Angel' pouch doll

A small change in the pattern gives a doll which appears to have arms or wings.

Materials and instructions are the same as for the pouch doll except that the wider body pattern below is used. It is best to use a fine cotton fabric which will gather easily.

5. Cut a small hole in the centre of the body piece, turn to right side and stuff with sheepswool. Put enough stuffing to make the body firm but still soft to the touch.

When you have made the doll as far as the end of #5, pull the two sides of the body into the centre. Thread a needle with a doubled length of thread and starting at X, with a few stitches to secure, take the needle through the body from X to X several times.

6. Put the completed head into the body and, starting at centre back of the body, make a line of running stitches. Turn in the raw edges of the body fabric at neck edge as you go. This means the stitches will go through two layers of fabric. Pull up the thread so the body fits snugly round the neck, then sew the head to the body using small stitches.

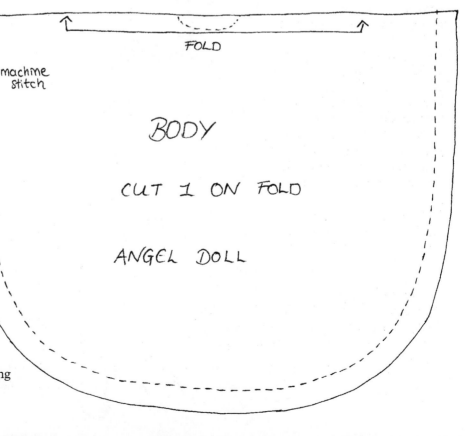

FOLD

machine stitch

BODY

CUT 1 ON FOLD

ANGEL DOLL

Adjust the gathers as you please and then fasten off. The position of these Xs can be altered to give a different look to the doll – experiment to see what you like best.

This doll can be made into an attractive gift for an adult by adding a little bag of pot pourri in matching fabric, perhaps with a lace trim to hat and bag.

Dolls house doll

This doll is 4″ (10cm) tall and has pipecleaners inside to form a framework so the doll can sit down. It is only suitable for older children. You can adapt the design to make a soft doll for a younger child by omitting the pipe-cleaners and making the body from soft fabric such as velour or flannelette.

Materials

Head – see previous instructions, page 39. It is easier to add the hair after sewing the head to the body.
3 pipe-cleaners (6″ [15cm] long) or thin covered wire
Cotton knit skin fabric 10″ x 5″ (25cm x 13cm)
Sheepswool ¹/₂ -1oz (15 - 25 gm)
Sewing thread
Embroidery cotton
Scraps of fabric for clothes

Instructions

1. Take one pipecleaner to form the arms and bend the ends over by 1¹/₄″ (3cm). The finished length is 3¹/₂″ (9cm).

ARMS

bend over

2. To make the legs, bend *LEGS* over one end on each of two pipecleaners by 1″ (2.5cm). Make a twist in the two remaining pipecleaners to hold them together 2½″ (6cm) from the bent (foot) end.

Fasten to the centre of the arms by bending the top part of the leg pipecleaners over the one used for the arms.

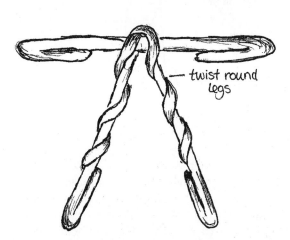

bend legs over arms

bend over

3. Twist the separate ends round each leg to secure. Check for size by holding against the actual size pattern given and adjust as necessary.

twist round legs

4. Wind carded sheepswool around this frame-work. Tuck an end of wool under the folded

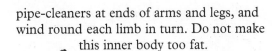

pipe-cleaners at ends of arms and legs, and wind round each limb in turn. Do not make this inner body too fat.

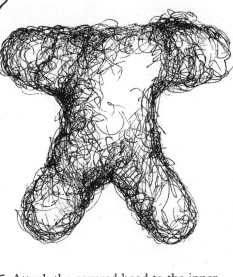

5. Attach the covered head to the inner body. To do this slit the sides of the material below the neck at each side and slip over the pipe-cleaner framework. You may find it necessary to open up the inner head below the neck as well. The head should sit firmly on the wire framework. Hold in place with a few stitches below the arms.

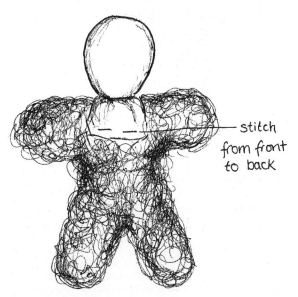

stitch from front to back

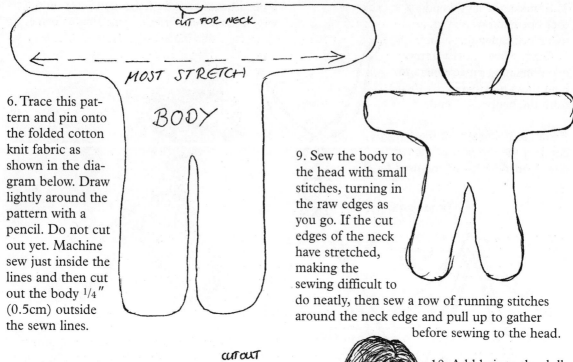

6. Trace this pattern and pin onto the folded cotton knit fabric as shown in the diagram below. Draw lightly around the pattern with a pencil. Do not cut out yet. Machine sew just inside the lines and then cut out the body ¼″ (0.5cm) outside the sewn lines.

9. Sew the body to the head with small stitches, turning in the raw edges as you go. If the cut edges of the neck have stretched, making the sewing difficult to do neatly, then sew a row of running stitches around the neck edge and pull up to gather before sewing to the head.

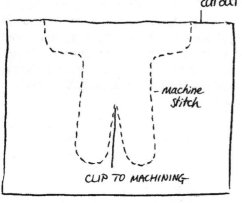

10. Add hair to the doll as described previously on page 41.

7. Cut a small hole for the neck at the centre of the body, as marked on the pattern, and snip close to the sewn line under the arms and between the legs.

8. Turn to the right side and gently insert the pipecleaner framework into the body. Add a little more stuffing, if necessary, by pushing small pieces of wool to the right spot with the blunt end of a slim pencil or thin dowel. Tweezers can also be useful to reach to the tips of legs and arms.

Clothes

These dolls are very small and will be overwhelmed by clothes that are too fussy or made from inappropriate material. Choose fabric that is thin, does not fray easily and is plain or has a small pattern. If you use pinking shears to cut out the clothes then the edges and hems can be left unfinished. No exact amounts have been given for the clothes, as only tiny scraps are needed.

Tabard dress

Cut out the dress according to the pattern given, using pinking shears, if you can, to minimise fraying, put the dress on the doll and tie at the waist with a narrow ribbon.

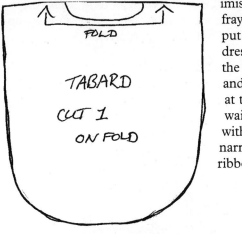

Starting at the centre front and using embroidery thread, sew a line of running stitches round the top of the skirt. Knot each end of the thread, draw up to fit the doll and tie with a bow.

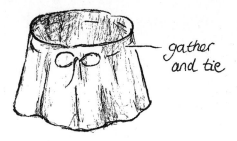

gather and tie

Skirt

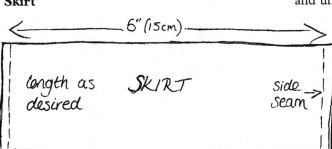

This can be made from a piece of ribbon of the right width or from a narrow strip of fabric.

Cut a 6″ (15cm) length of fabric or ribbon, the width can be varied to give the length of skirt desired.

Top or dress

Using the full size pattern below, cut out the shirt on the fold of the material. Sew the side and underarm seams on the wrong side of the material. Hem the bottom edge if you wish. Turn the dress to the right side. Starting at the centre front, sew a row of running stitches around the neck opening with embroidery thread. Knot both ends of the embroidery thread, put on the doll and draw up to fit the doll. Finish by tying with a bow.

Sew the two short ends together on the wrong side and turn to right side. Hem the bottom edge if you wish.

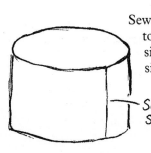

side seam

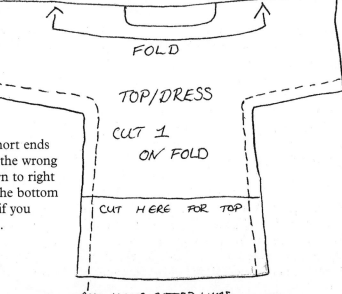

Trousers

Cut out two trouser pieces using the actual size pattern pieces.

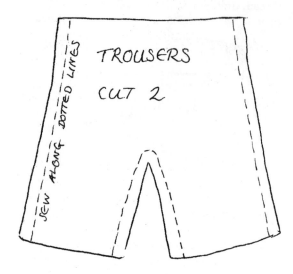

Place the wrong sides together and sew the centre front and centre back seams, then sew the leg seam from one side to the other. Hem the bottoms of the legs if you wish.

Turn the trousers to the right side and put on the doll. If they do not fit snugly at the top use embroidery thread to sew a line of running stitches round the waist. Knot this at each end, pull up to fit and tie in a bow.

Waistcoat

A full size pattern is given. Cut out the waistcoat and sew the shoulder seams. This is best made out of felt and can be decorated with a little embroidery.

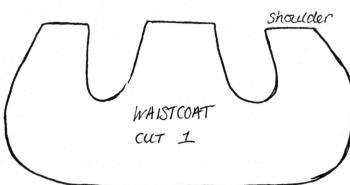

Knitted clothes

Simple knitted clothes can be made using 3 or 4 ply wool (sportsweight) and fine needles. Make squares and rectangles to fit, using the patterns given for fabric as a guide, and sew up to make a top, skirt, or trousers.

Doll with hands

This doll is made in a different way although it still uses the same size head.

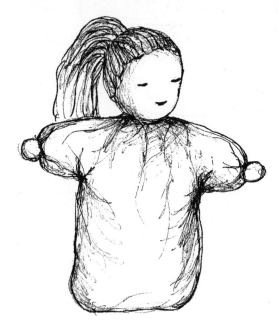

Materials

Inner head – follow instructions #1, #2 and #3 given for simple head.
Cotton knit skin fabric 6″ x 4″ (15cm x 10cm)
Fabric for body 6″ x 10″ (15cm x 25cm)
Sheepswool 1 - 2oz (25 - 50gm)
Sewing thread
Strong thread or thin crochet cotton
Yarn or embroidery thread (floss) for hair

Instructions

1. Lay out the cotton knit fabric and place the inner head on it centrally as shown in the diagram.

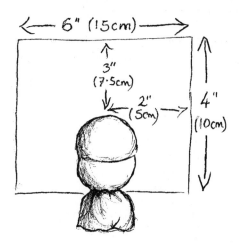

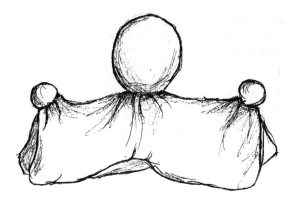

2. Fold over the top half of the knit fabric and, holding the head below the neck with one hand, gather the fabric round the head. Stretch over the head so that there are as few folds and gathers as possible. Tie around the neck with strong cotton.

4. Using the pattern given below on page 50 cut out a body piece. The material should be folded with the right sides together and the pattern placed on the folded edge of the fabric.

With right sides together sew the seam on the body as shown on the pattern.

5. Cut a small hole in the centre of the body piece, turn to right side and stuff with sheepswool.

6. Put the head and hands inside the body via the neck. Adjust stuffing if necessary. Sew the fabric at the neck to the head and at the wrists to hands, turning in the raw edges as you go.

7. Add features and hair to the head as explained in the instructions on pages 40 - 41.

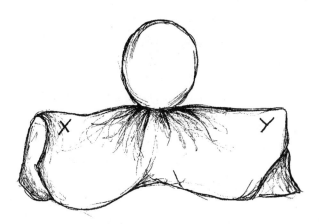

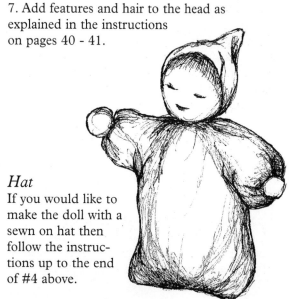

3. To make the hands take a tiny piece of sheepswool and roll into a ball. Tie the cotton knit fabric round this at the furthest point from the head (marked with an X in the picture). Repeat on the other side (Y) to make the second hand.

Hat

If you would like to make the doll with a sewn on hat then follow the instructions up to the end of #4 above.

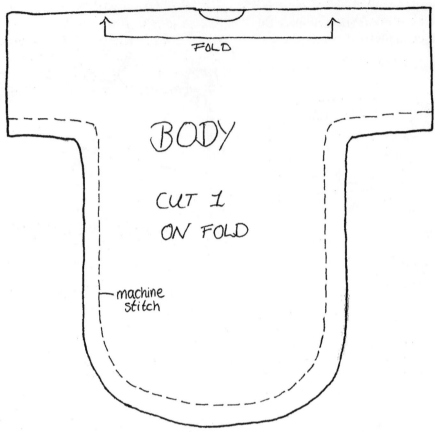

FOLD

BODY

CUT 1
ON FOLD

machine
stitch

Then use the pattern for the hat belonging to the pouch doll. Cut out and sew the hat seam, add features and hair following instructions on pages 40 - 41. Sew the hat to the head as described for the pouch doll. Insert the head, complete with hat, into the neck opening, ensuring the unfinished, lower edges of the hat are hidden inside the body.

Continue sewing the doll, following the instructions from #5 onwards above.

Doll with hands and feet

This is a variation of the doll with hands. The materials needed are the same – except for a larger piece of cotton knit fabric, 6″ x 12″ (15cm x 30cm).

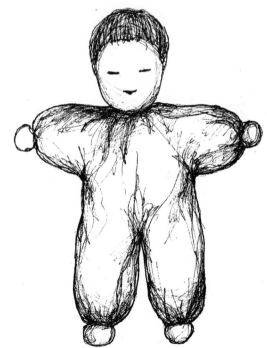

1. Lay out the cotton knit fabric and place the inner head in the centre of the top part of the fabric as shown in the diagram.

2. Fold over the top 2½″ (6cm) of the cotton knit fabric and, holding the head below the neck with one hand, gather the fabric round the head. Stretch the cotton knit over the head so that there are as few folds and gathers as possible. Tie around the neck with strong thread.

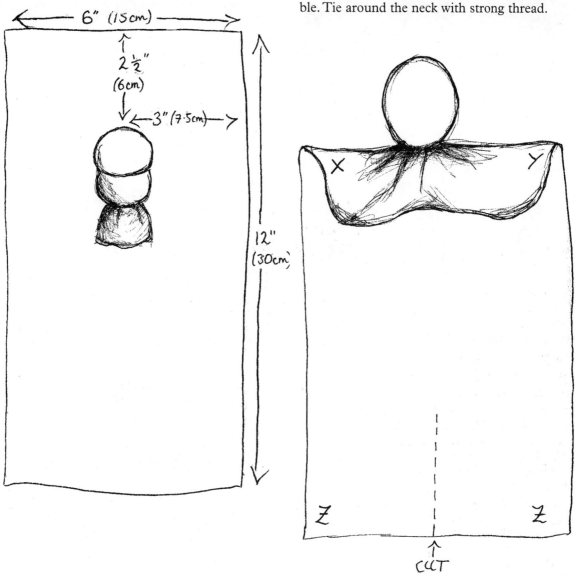

3. To make the hands take a tiny piece of sheepswool and roll into a ball. Tie the cotton knit fabric round this at the point marked X on the picture. Repeat on the other side (Y) to make the second hand.

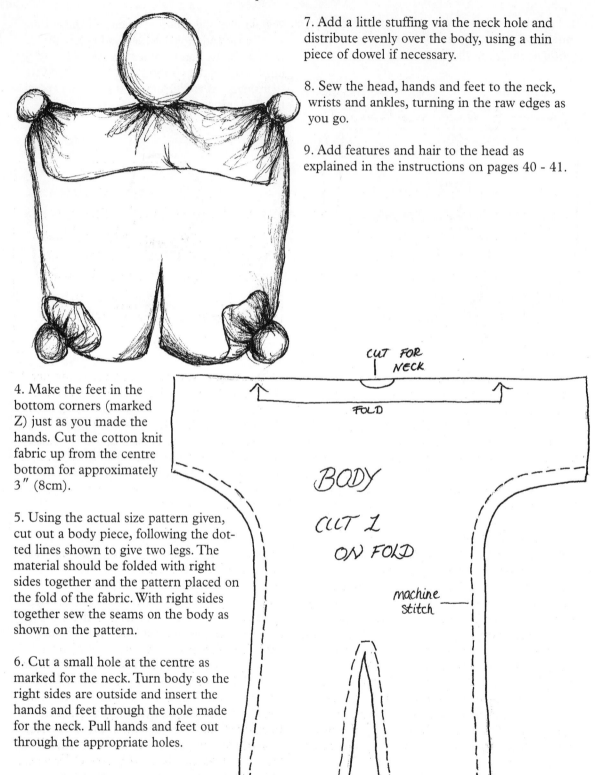

7. Add a little stuffing via the neck hole and distribute evenly over the body, using a thin piece of dowel if necessary.

8. Sew the head, hands and feet to the neck, wrists and ankles, turning in the raw edges as you go.

9. Add features and hair to the head as explained in the instructions on pages 40 - 41.

4. Make the feet in the bottom corners (marked Z) just as you made the hands. Cut the cotton knit fabric up from the centre bottom for approximately 3″ (8cm).

5. Using the actual size pattern given, cut out a body piece, following the dotted lines shown to give two legs. The material should be folded with right sides together and the pattern placed on the fold of the fabric. With right sides together sew the seams on the body as shown on the pattern.

6. Cut a small hole at the centre as marked for the neck. Turn body so the right sides are outside and insert the hands and feet through the hole made for the neck. Pull hands and feet out through the appropriate holes.

CUT FOR NECK

FOLD

BODY

CUT 1 ON FOLD

machine stitch

Chapter 4

Soft Dolls

Soft squashy dolls with fabric bodies are perfect first toys. Made from velour or brushed cotton they are wonderful to hold and cuddle, with simple faces and hands. The doll emerging from soft bundles of fabric is a mirror of the child's own movement from babyhood to becoming a child. Soft dolls are very practical too – they wash easily and because they contain less stuffing will dry quickly – hats and hands are often chewed by little mouths so must be sewn very safely.

For the youngest baby a simple doll made from a piece of cloth knotted and tied to give the impression of a head and hands is all that is needed. It is the adult who feels the doll is not finished because there are no features. The lack of precise form in the limbs is exactly right for this developmental stage. The baby is interested in the colour and texture of the toy and maybe also if it is easy to chew!

Sometimes older children who are unfamiliar with these simple dolls are also attracted to them. I made one of these first dolls for a friend who had just had a baby. Her older child, a 6-year-old named Jenny, who had previously only owned commercially manufactured dolls, immediately adopted it as her own. This did not seem to be simply a case of sibling jealousy because other gifts were ignored and when Jenny was offered her own simple doll she happily gave the baby his doll back. Jenny made a soft bed for her new baby, wrapped it in a shawl and looked after it tenderly for many months, with scarcely a glance at her more sophisticated dolls.

As the baby grows and its limbs start to uncurl and make contact with the world it is ready for a doll with a little more form. The pouch doll included in the **Small Dolls** chapter has a head with features and some hair but a soft rounded body with little detail. The small child sitting in the buggy or baby carrier will feel happy clutching one of these dolls, for there is a face to look at and a soft body to hug.

A child's first drawings of people concentrate on the face and its features just as the emphasis on these dolls is in the face.

As the baby grows into a toddler and learns to walk, run and climb he or she also starts to talk, and with the beginning of language then imaginative play can grow and develop to a greater extent than before. Toddlers appreciate the more formed dolls shown in this chapter, either the baggy doll or the sack doll. A slightly older child will like a more detailed doll – perhaps sewn from sturdy corduroy or cotton with a brightly coloured waistcoat or dress. This doll can also be given a fully shaped head with a closely sewn cap of hair. A doll can have another function now –

it also becomes a security blanket – to hug when life gets too much and to cuddle at bedtime.

Freddie was an energetic boy who rushed from one toy to another, never settling for more than a few minutes and he seemed to take great delight in refusing to do any activity suggested by adults. His grandmother decided to make him a sack doll. She chose green corduroy and sewed a doll with legs and arms and a formed head with brown embroidered hair. She made a waistcoat from a bright piece of felt and hand knitted a hat and scarf in rainbow stripes. Next time she went to visit her grandson, then aged three and a half, she took the doll along. She sat the doll beside her on the sofa but said nothing. Freddie charged around playing with various toys and finally noticed the doll.

'What's that? Who's it for? Can I have dolly?' then, without waiting for an answer, he picked it up and started throwing it in the air. Granny caught the doll and placed it back on the sofa. She sat Freddie on her lap and told him a story about a doll, called Tom, who was wandering all over the city looking for a place to live. Tom just couldn't find the right place – one house was too busy, another had no children to care for him, yet another too noisy and so on. Freddie became quite excited saying 'Here, here, dolly stay here'. Granny said she didn't know if it would be a good place but perhaps if Freddie wanted to try to look after the doll then she could try leaving him for a little while. She reminded Freddie that Tom was very young and needed lots of quiet times and plenty of sleep. He nodded solemnly and went to fetch his tip-up truck to give Tom a ride. Freddie played with doll for nearly 20 minutes, an extraordinarily long time for him, and when he turned to play with another toy he told his Granny 'Tom tired now' and put him gently on the sofa to sleep.

On subsequent visits Freddie was quick to reassure Granny that Tom loved living with him and had found the right house now. Freddie's mother reported that he continued to play with

Tom for extended periods and sometimes if his play was too noisy or too unfocused then she would suggest that Tom looked bored and might like to do some other activity such as going for a walk or drawing a picture. Freddie found it much easier to agree 'for Tom' than to accept the suggestion for himself. All this happened several years ago and Freddie is now a very grown up nine-year-old who thinks himself much too old to play with dolls. However Tom still lives in Freddie's bedroom where he is hidden from sight, pushed down inside the bedclothes, so Freddie's feet can be in close contact all night.

Materials

Colour and texture of the fabric used is of great importance. A young child just emerging from babyhood needs gentle colours: white, cream, pink, lilac or pale blue. Plain or self-coloured fabric with a soft texture is most appropriate for this age – it should not detract from the gentle form of the doll.

A doll made for an older toddler can be sewn from fabric with a colour which appeals to the child's temperament and general mood. I can only give a brief guide to colours here, but spend a few moments thinking about your child and what colour they respond to.

An outgoing or strong willed child will respond to a red doll because red energises, stimulates and gives confidence. Blue is relaxing and peaceful; it will be appreciated by a thoughtful boy or girl. Green is a harmonious colour and can encourage giving and sharing, while pink or lilac is restful and calming. Yellow often excites and animates children, which is not too good for a quiet bedtime.

When choosing fabric for your doll take time to feel it, hold it to your face until you find a pleasant texture. On a practical note the fabric must be washable and hard-wearing – this doll is going to be well loved and can expect to travel to all sorts of places. Fabric made from natural fibres is best both for aesthetic and practical reasons.

Before you begin please read the chapter **General Techniques** which has notes on basic stitches and other important points about doll-making. Note especially the information on the variability of sheepswool; and that the quantities given here are only guidelines.

Baggy doll

A soft doll with a rounded one-piece body and baggy arms, it has a just-got-out-of-bed look and makes a perfect night-time companion for a small child. It is smaller and quicker to make than the sack doll described later and is constructed in a simpler way.

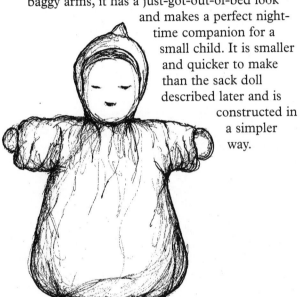

Materials

10″ (25cm) tubular gauze stockinette, flat measurement 1¹⁄₂″ (2.5cm)
or
A piece of T-shirt material 7″ x 5¹⁄₂″ (18cm x 14cm), sewn into a tube 7″ x 2³⁄₄″ (18cm x 7cm)
4oz (100gm) sheepswool
Cotton knit skin fabric 10″ x 12″ (25cm x 30cm)
Soft fabric for body – velour, brushed cotton etc. 20″ x 24″ (50cm x 60cm)
Sewing cotton to match body fabric and hair
Embroidery thread for features
Yarn – small quantity for hair
Crochet cotton or thin string
Small bell (*optional*)

Making the head
Method

1. Cut a small piece of crochet cotton and tie the tube near the top of one end. Turn so the knot is on the inside.

2. Stuff with 1¹⁄₂ - 2 oz (35 - 50gm) of sheepswool. The finished shape is 6″ (15cm) long by 2¹⁄₂″ (7cm) across and 7″ (18cm) round. Mould the tubing with your hands as you stuff to get this shape. Gather together the bottom edges of the tube and secure with crochet cotton. Tie with a bow, as you need to undo this later. The upper part of the stuffed tube forms the head.

3. Use your hands to make the neck by first squeezing the tube 2¹⁄₂″ (7cm) from the top and then tie with crochet cotton. The head should have a rounded look – not too long and thin.

neck

4. Cut a piece of crochet thread 20″ (50cm) long and make the eyeline by wrapping the thread tightly round the head twice and knotting firmly. The eyeline is about halfway down the head. Cut off the loose threads.

5. Undo the string at the bottom of the head and gently remove some of the stuffing, then retie. Unless you do this there will be a hard lump at the centre of the doll inside an otherwise soft and squashy body.

Head covering

1. Cut out the head covering and arms from the pattern allowing an extra 1/2" (1cm) all round for the seam allowance. The arms and head are made from skin-coloured cotton. As they both have to be cut on the fold of the fabric you may find it easier to cut the head covering first and then refold the fabric before cutting the arms.

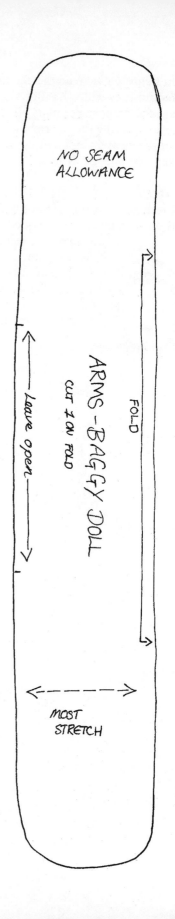

NO SEAM ALLOWANCE

Leave open

ARMS – BAGGY DOLL

CUT 1 ON FOLD

FOLD

MOST STRETCH

HEAD COVERING
BAGGY DOLL

CUT 1 ON FOLD

FOLD

NO SEAM ALLOWANCE

MOST STRETCH

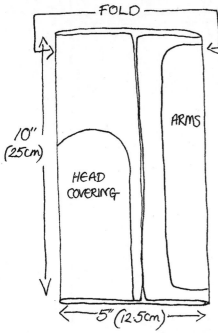

2. Machine the head covering along the top and side, leaving the bottom open. Turn the head covering inside out and put over the inner head. The knot on the eyeline string and the seam on the head covering should both be at the back of the head.

machine stitch

3. Tie around the neck with crochet cotton keeping the skin fabric taut round the head.

4. Take 3 glass-headed pins and mark the positions of the eyes and mouth. The eyes are placed on the eye string about

1″ (2.5cm) apart. The mouth is placed halfway between the eyes and 3/4″ (1.5cm) below.

5. Using a long needle and appropriately coloured embroidery thread sew the eyes and mouth. Fasten the thread at the back of the head and bring the needle through to one side of a pin marking the eye. Take a straight stitch over the pin and then make another in exactly the same place, bringing the threaded needle out to the back of the head. Repeat for the second eye.

mouth The mouth is sewn in the same way but is made up of one long stitch and a second shorter one directly below the first.

Hair

1. Measure across the front of the doll's head from ear to ear and wind off a small hank of yarn this length.

2. Sew to head with matching sewing cotton; put a double row of running stitches at the two sides and at the centre of the yarn.

Other ideas for hairstyles can be found in Chapter 2. A partial version (i.e. only at the front) of the knitted or the 'pins and loops' style looks good and is safe as there are no loose ends to be pulled or chewed.

Body and hat

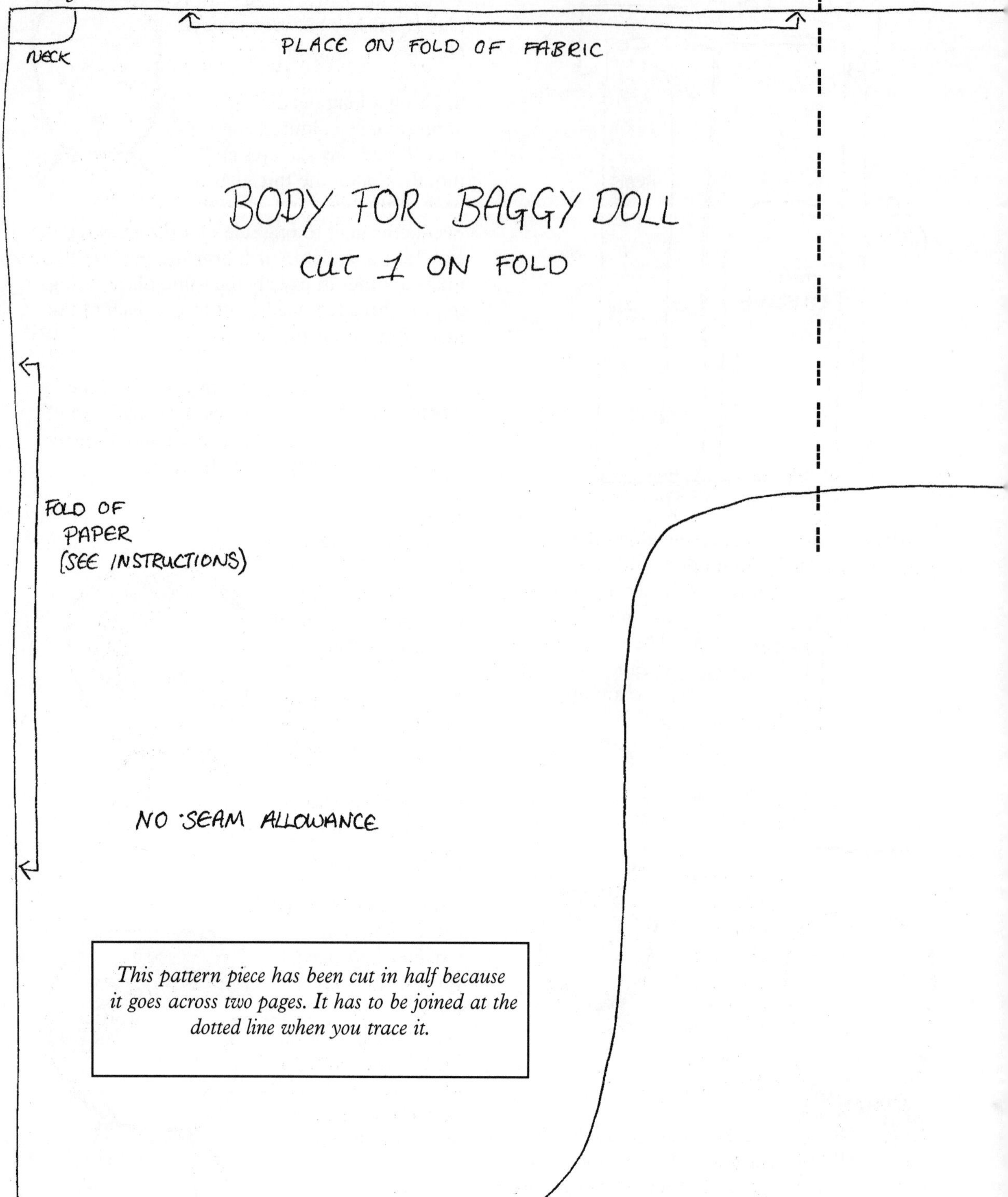

NECK

PLACE ON FOLD OF FABRIC

BODY FOR BAGGY DOLL
CUT 1 ON FOLD

FOLD OF
PAPER
(SEE INSTRUCTIONS)

NO SEAM ALLOWANCE

> *This pattern piece has been cut in half because it goes across two pages. It has to be joined at the dotted line when you trace it.*

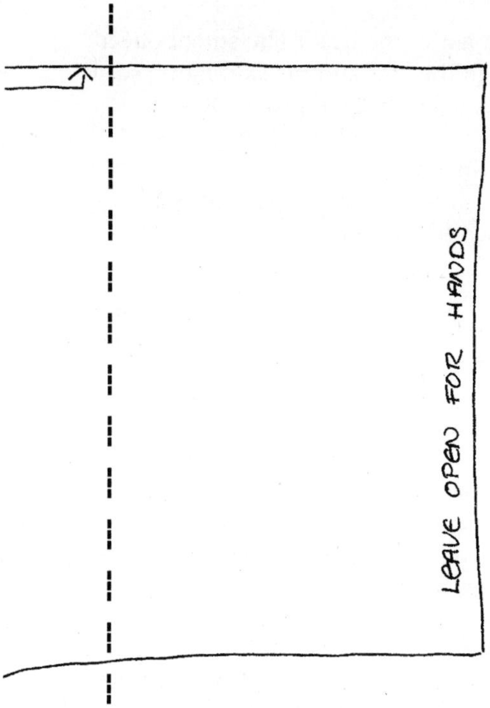

LEAVE OPEN FOR HANDS

1. Pattern

Trace the hat and body pieces from the pattern given. Only half of the body pattern is shown – to make a complete pattern, fold a large sheet of paper in half and trace the shape shown onto one side. Cut the pattern out with the paper folded and you should now have a complete, full-sized body pattern.

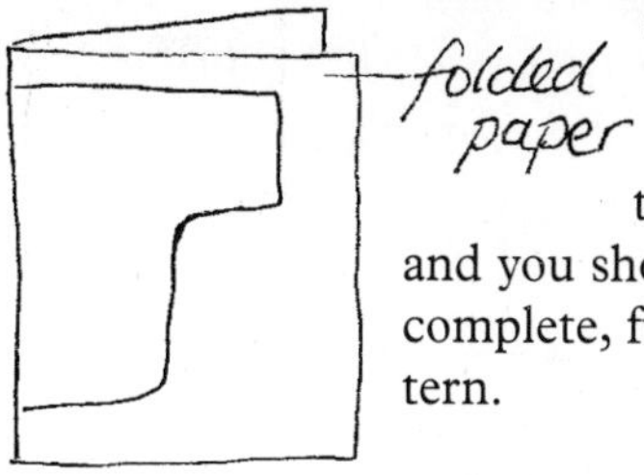

folded paper

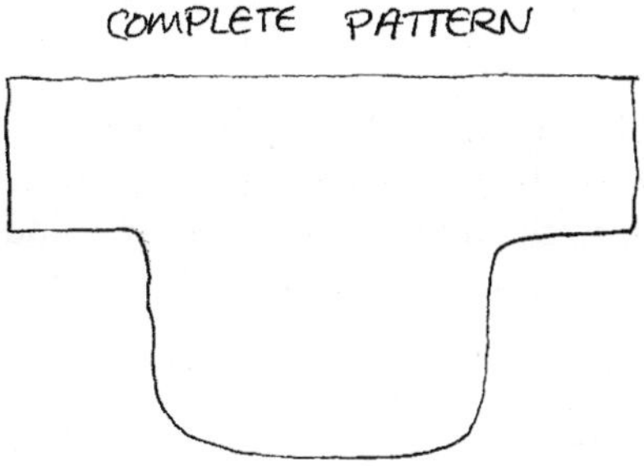

COMPLETE PATTERN

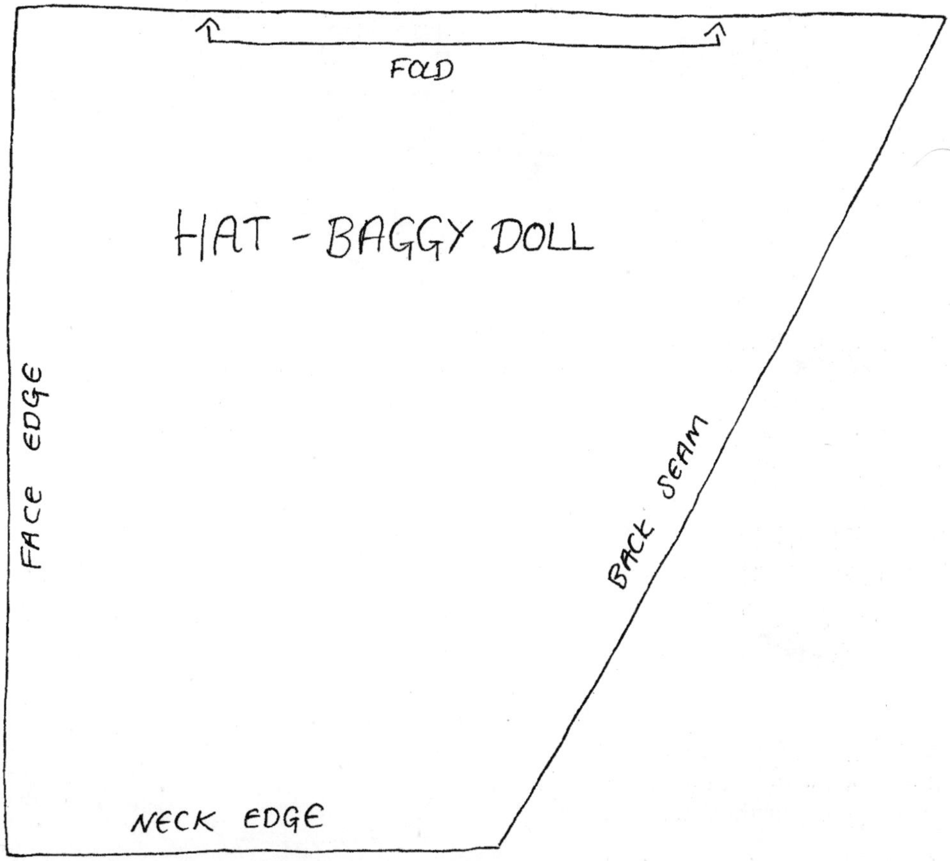

FOLD

HAT - BAGGY DOLL

FACE EDGE

BACK SEAM

NECK EDGE

2. Place the body and hat pieces on your chosen material as shown in the diagram and cut out, adding ½" (1cm) on all the cut edges for a seam allowance.

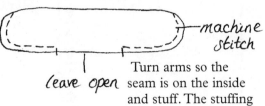

10" (25cm)

BODY   HAT

23½ (60cm)

3. With the right sides of the material together, sew the body in a continuous seam from one arm to the other, leaving the arm ends open.

machine stitch

bell   machine stitch   Sew the back seam of the hat.

4. Hat
Turn hat so the right sides are outside. A bell can be added now, but sew it firmly on to the seam allowance inside the hat. It will still jingle merrily but with no danger of being removed and swallowed.

tie round neck

Put the hat on the doll's head with the seam at the back. Tie around the neck with sewing cotton. Turn under the raw edges near the face

and sew the hat to the head. The stitches need to go through the hair and the skin fabric so everything is held firmly in place.

5. Arms and hands
Sew the arm piece leaving the centre 3" (8cm) open for stuffing.

machine stitch

leave open

Turn arms so the seam is on the inside and stuff. The stuffing needs to be harder at the ends (hands) and softer at the centre where this piece will be attached to the body. Close the gap at the centre with a few stitches.

Place the stuffed arms centrally, at the front, on the lower part of the inner head (the muff) and sew in place with several stab stitches.

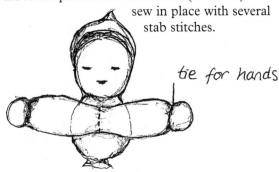

tie for hands

6. Body
Cut a small hole, as indicated, at the centre of the body for the neck. Turn so right side of fabric is outside. Stuff the body quite firmly, but leave the arms empty.

cut for neck

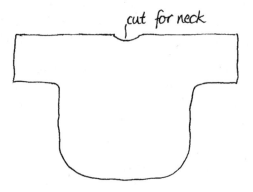

Insert the arms and then the head into the body via the neck opening. If this is difficult because the opening does not stretch enough, then remove the head and enlarge the neck a little. Try to keep the neck hole as small as possible otherwise it may look untidy when sewn.

Pull the hands through the arms and check the stuffing is in the right place so the doll is cuddly with no hollow spots. Add extra wool if necessary.

The body pattern is cut so that the arm is longer than the inner arm/hand piece and when gathered and sewn at the wrist the sleeve is loose and baggy.

Sew a row of running stitches round the neck opening, turning the raw edges in as you go. Gather the neck edge to fit the head and sew (catch or hem stitch) the head to the body, making sure that at least half the stitches go through all the layers of fabric.

With matching sewing thread tie the arms about 1″ (2.5cm) from the ends to make the hands.

gathering thread

ARM

Sew a gathering thread round the edge of the arms, turning the raw edge in as you go. Pull up this thread so the two pieces (hands and arms) meet at the wrist and sew together firmly.

Sack dolls

Sack dolls are cuddly dolls which have a clearer body shape than the baggy dolls but are still soft and largely unformed. They are suitable for toddlers and, in their more developed state with arms, legs and a head of hair, for children of five or more.

The inner head and body are made together and the outer body – with either a bag or legs for the lower part – is made from fabric. The face and hands are made from skin-coloured cotton knit fabric, with a sewn on cap to match the body.

The basic proportions of this doll are based on the head, which is one quarter of the doll. The arms and torso make up another quarter, and the remaining half is taken up with the lower body (including the legs).

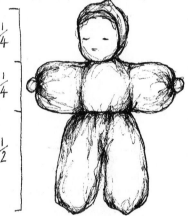

$\frac{1}{4}$

$\frac{1}{4}$

$\frac{1}{2}$

Materials
1½″ (4cm) wide stretch tubing 10″ (25cm) long
or
Rectangle of T-shirt fabric (cotton knit fabric) 6″ x 9″ (15cm x 23cm), sewn into a tube 3″ x 9″ (8cm x 23cm)
¼yd (25cm) cotton knit in a skin colour.
½yd (50cm) fabric for the body – e.g. cotton velour, brushed cotton or flannelette, corduroy or medium weight cotton.
Knitting wool for hair
8oz (250gm) sheepswool for stuffing.
Embroidery thread in colours appropriate for the features
Sewing thread to match skin fabric and body fabric
Strong thick thread or mercerised cotton crochet cotton (2yd [2m])

Method

Inner head and body

Cotton tubing is the easiest material to use as it has no seam and stretches uniformly across its width, but it may be difficult to obtain in small quantities in the size required. An acceptable alternative is to make your own tube by sewing a seam along one side of a folded rectangle of light coloured cotton knit or T-shirt fabric. The grain or knit lines go down the length of the tube with the most stretch across the tube.

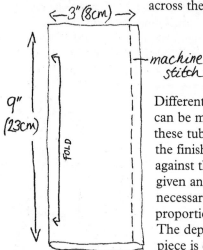

←—3" (8cm) —→

├—*machine stitch*

9" (23cm)

FOLD

Different sizes of head can be made from these tubes – measure the finished head against the pattern given and adapt as necessary to keep the proportions correct. The depth of the arm piece is equal to the height of the head, and the lower body equal to twice the head height. Thus if the doll's head (measured from the neck to top of head) is 4″ (10cm) high then the arms will be 4″ (10cm) deep and the lower body 8″ (20cm). The width of the pattern pieces and the hat also need to be adjusted to keep the proportions pleasing to the eye.

Making the head

1. Cut a short piece of strong cotton thread and tie the tubing at the top. Turn so the top raw edges are inside.

2. Stuff with sheepswool. The final size of the stuffed tube is 7″ (18cm) long, 3″ (7.5cm) wide and 10″ (25cm) round the circumference. You must keep pulling and moulding the

tube into shape otherwise it will get too short and wide. The inner head needs to be stuffed quite firmly and should take 4oz (100gm) of your wool. Gather the bottom edges of the tube and fasten with strong thread. Tie with a bow, as you will undo this string later.

←—*neck*

tie with bow at bottom

The top part of the sausage shape becomes the head and the lower part the body.

3. Use your hands to mould the neck by squeezing and massaging the wool 3″ (7.5cm) from the top of the head. When you have a clear indentation for the neck then tie round with strong thread. Wrap the thread round the neck twice, pull hard and tie the ends of thread together firmly. The finished head shape should be rounded, not long and narrow.

Shaping the head

4. The eyeline is made with a piece of thread tied halfway down the head to mark the position of the eyes.

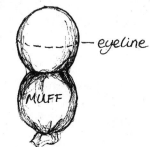

—*eyeline*

MUFF

Take a length of strong thread 40″ (100cm) long and start at one side of the head. Leave a short length of thread hanging down and, holding this in place with your thumb, wrap the thread round the head twice. Pull quite hard on the thread so there is a clear indentation. Knot the threads together at your starting place at the side of the head. The position of the knot roughly corresponds to the position of an ear on the head.

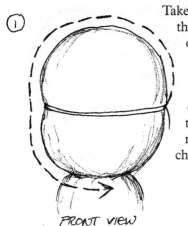

① Take the longer thread, bring over the top of the head (1), and down, crossing the eye string, to the neck at the middle of the chin.

FRONT VIEW

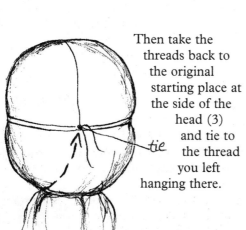

② Now take the thread once right round the neck (2) and back to the mid point under the chin.

— wrap around neck

③ Then take the threads back to the original starting place at the side of the head (3) and tie to the thread you left hanging there.

tie

Finally, to stop these threads moving out of place in the future, sew across them at the sides of the head. Use a strong thread and sew an X where the eyestring and chin string meet at

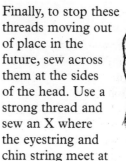

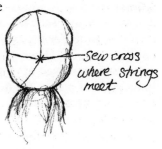

—Sew cross where strings meet

each side of the head. Make sure that your needle goes a little way into the head itself so everything is held together securely.

Check your head against the actual size drawing shown here. The patterns for the body are based on a head with these measurements and will need to be altered if your head is much bigger or smaller.

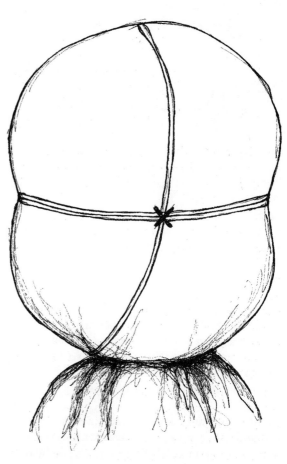

Adjust stuffing in lower head

The inner body below the neck has to be firmly stuffed in order for the neck and head to be correctly tied off. However, some stuffing now needs to be removed or else it will form a hard lump at the centre of the doll. Undo the bottom of the inner head and carefully take out about half of the stuffing below the neck. Do not disturb any pieces of fleece that come down through the neck or else it will become floppy. Refasten securely with some thin cotton string or crochet thread.

Head covering and hands

1. Cut a rectangle of cotton knit skin fabric 8″ (20cm) square. Fold in half so that the most stretch goes across the fabric.

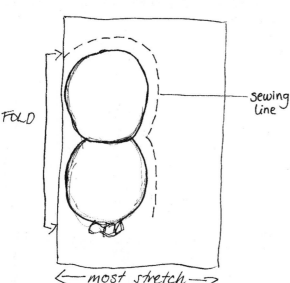

FOLD

— sewing line

← most stretch →

2. Put head on the fabric with front of head touching the fold of the material and draw around as shown in the diagram. This line will be your sewing line. Cut out leaving a ¹/₂″ (1cm) seam allowance. Machine around the head covering, leaving bottom open.

3. Turn the skin coloured head cover right side out and put over the inner head with the seam at the back. Pull gently into place and tie with

cotton string around the neck so that the covering fits snugly over the head.

4. Cut two circles of skin fabric for the hands, each circle measures 3″ (8cm) across. Put aside until later.

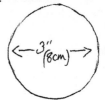

<--- 3″(8cm) --->

tie at neck

Face and hair

1. Mark the features with glass-headed pins. Aim for an equilateral triangle with evenly spaced features. The eyes are on the eye string and mouth below.

2. Sew the eyes and mouth. Use a long needle and the appropriate coloured embroidery thread. Start and finish at the back and side of the head. The eyes need two small straight stitches one on top of the other. The mouth consists of one stitch across with a smaller one directly underneath.

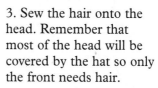

— mouth

3. Sew the hair onto the head. Remember that most of the head will be covered by the hat so only the front needs hair.

The simplest hairstyle is to arrange lengths of wool across the front of the head and sew down at the sides and centre with

matching sewing thread. Alternative ideas can be found in Chapter 2 on hair.

Arms, body, legs and hat

1. Trace off the actual size patterns given for the hat and body. You have the option of making the lower part of the body as a sack or with legs. I prefer to use the sack for younger children and legs for older ones but it is not an invariable rule as much depends on the texture of the fabric being used.

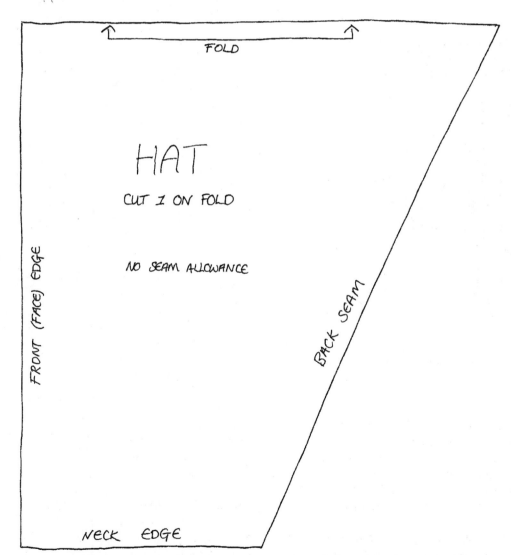

FOLD

HAT

CUT 1 ON FOLD

NO SEAM ALLOWANCE

FRONT (FACE) EDGE

BACK SEAM

NECK EDGE

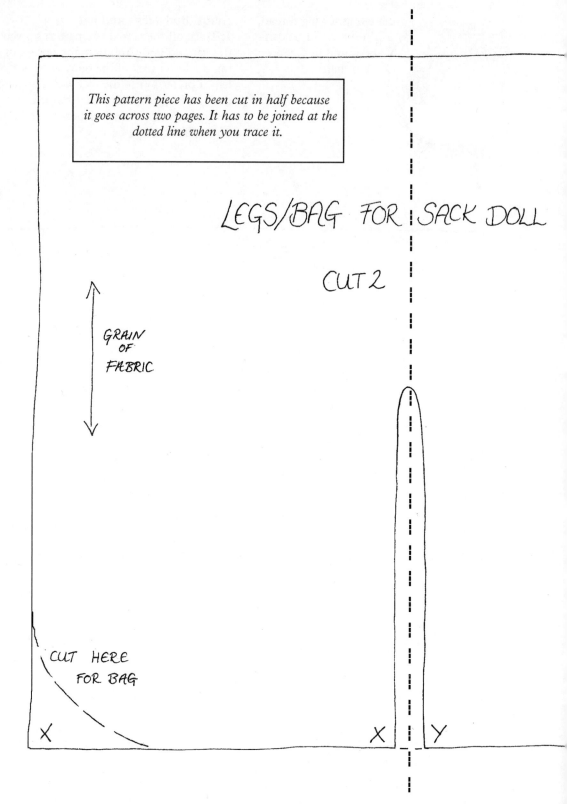

This pattern piece has been cut in half because it goes across two pages. It has to be joined at the dotted line when you trace it.

LEGS/BAG FOR SACK DOLL

CUT 2

GRAIN
OF
FABRIC

CUT HERE
FOR BAG

X

X   Y

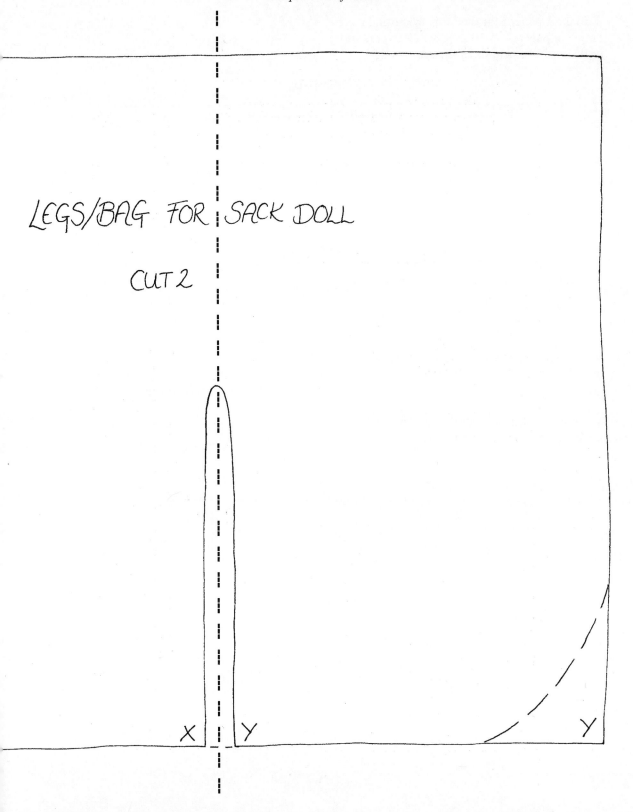

LEGS/BAG FOR SACK DOLL

CUT 2

X   Y

Y

2. Make a pattern for the arms by cutting a rectangle of paper 3″ x 10½″ (8cm x 27cm) and write on the directions as shown.

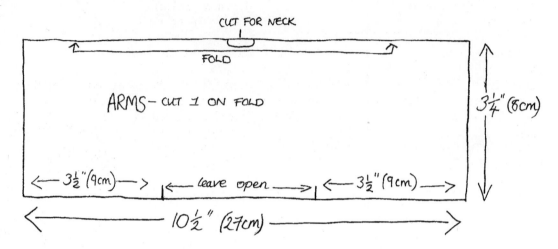

3. Lay out the pattern pieces on the fabric noting which pieces need to be cut out on a fold etc.

Draw round the pattern pieces and cut out ½″ (1cm) outside this line. The line you have drawn will be your sewing line.

Velour and other knit fabrics must have the most stretch going across the patterns.

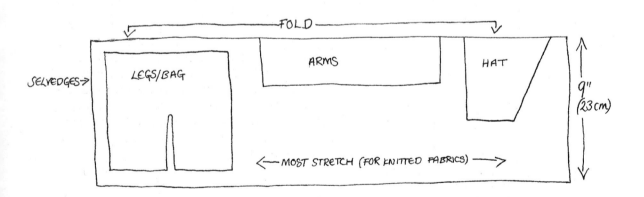

4. Sew, preferably by machine, as indicated on the pattern and as shown in the diagram.

Arms and upper body

Fold fabric with right sides together, machine underarm seam leaving the centre third open.

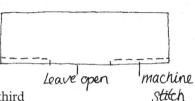

Lower body – sack

With right sides of fabric together sew all round the lower edges leaving the waist seam open.

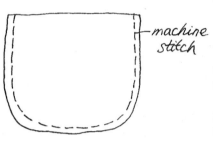

Lower body – legs

Sew around the lower body as shown leaving the bottom of the legs open as well as the waist.

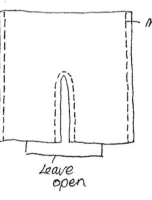

On each leg match the inside and outside seam (X to X) and (Y to Y) then machine across the bottom of the leg. This gives a more defined foot.

Hat

With right sides together machine the back (angled) seam of the hat.

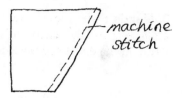

Making up the Doll

1. Hat

Turn the fabric hat so the seam is on the inside and place on the head with the seam at the back. Using a matching colour of sewing thread, tie firmly around the neck. Then, with a hemming stitch, sew the front of the hat to the head. Use a hemming stitch and turn the raw edge under as you go.

2. Arms

Cut a 2″ (5cm) hole in the centre of the arm piece at the neck and turn the arms to the right side. Start at the centre back and run a gathering thread (running stitch) around the opening, turning the raw edge under as you go. Slip the head through the neck and draw up the gathering thread. The raw edges at the bottom of the hat should be hidden inside the arm piece. Check that the gathers are evenly distributed around the neck and that the head faces to the front. Sew the head to the neck edge with small, neat stitches in the matching sewing thread.

Stuff arms with sheepswool. They should not be too floppy but feel about the same as the lower part of the inner head.

Run a gathering thread round the end of the arm, turning in the raw edge as you go.

3. Hands

Take one of the circles of skin fabric and place a small ball of stuffing in the centre. Draw fabric round to make a firm ball. Tie at the base with thread. Make another hand in the same way.

Insert hand into open arm, pull up the gathering thread to fit snugly round and sew the arm fabric to the hand.

Lower body
Sack: turn to right sides and stuff to match arms.

Legs: Snip fabric at crotch and turn to right sides and stuff to match arms.

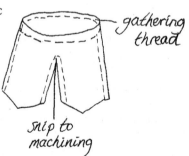

Sack and legs

1. Sew a gathering thread around the waist edge.

2. Place lower part of the inner body inside and pull up the thread. Check that the central portion of arm fabric will cover the waist seam.

3. Using large running stitches sew the sack or legs to the inner body at waist making sure that the side seams of the arms and lower body match.

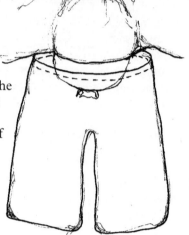

4. Sew the fabric at the centre between the arms at the back and front over the waist seam of the lower body or legs. Make these stitches as small and neat as possible.

Variations
Hat
This pattern can be adapted to have a longer point like a pixie's or a more rounded bonnet shape.

A small bell can be added, but for safety reasons sew this to the inside of the hat before sewing onto the head.

Hands
The patterns given for the arm of the medium jointed or traditional doll can be used if a more detailed hand is required. Use the hand part of the pattern plus about 2″ (5cm) of the arm. Cut out, machine and stuff as for the limbed doll, then sew into the gathered edge of the arm as described above.

Feet
Make these just like the hands – perhaps from slightly larger circles (4″ [10cm]). Cut out and sew as for the doll with legs but do not machine across the bottom, instead gather and sew in feet as for the hands. A more formed foot can be made following the pattern given for the medium jointed doll, cutting off the pattern about half way up the leg and sewing in the sole

as instructed. Stuff and sew to the gathered lower edge of the legs. Feet are more appropriate for a doll which is to be given to an older toddler – perhaps one which has a full head of hair as described below.

A fully formed head and hair

If a doll is to have a full head of hair then the back of the head needs more shaping than that of a doll with a sewn-on hat. These instructions are the same as for the limbed doll but are repeated below for convenience.

Method: Make the inner head as described on page 62 of this chapter to the end of number 4.

5. Pull the eye string at the back of the head down to meet the neck string. Massage the sheepswool so that it moves up if the strings are tight.

BACK OF HEAD

pull down

6. Thread a sturdy needle with strong crochet cotton or thin string and sew across the two lower strings to smooth out any bumps. The idea is not to draw the strings together but to flatten the lower

sew across

part of the head. It is like a large darning stitch. Repeat at the other side and fasten off.

Continue making the head covering and features as for the doll with a hat.

Cut out the body pieces and sew and assemble according to the direction given, ignoring all references to the hair and the hat. When the body of the doll, with hands and feet as desired, is finished then add the hair.

Read through Chapter 2 on hair to get ideas for different styles. A close fitting style is often more appropriate to this doll than long loose hair – it depends on the age of the child the doll is intended for.

Clothes

Simple styles are best – a brightly coloured waistcoat or vest adds plenty of character and is easy to take on and off. A gathered skirt will slip over the doll's bulky body easily and a knitted jacket or tunic also stretches to make dressing the doll simple.

Waistcoat (Vest)
Materials
Felt – needs no turning and does not fray
Medium weight cotton or wool fabric
Leather or suede
Only a small piece of fabric is needed
Sewing thread to match
Embroidery thread

Method: Cut out according to the full size pattern given on the next page adding $1/2''$ (1cm) seam allowance where necessary.

Place the shoulders with the right sides of the fabric together and sew the shoulder seams. Turn to right side.

sew at shoulders

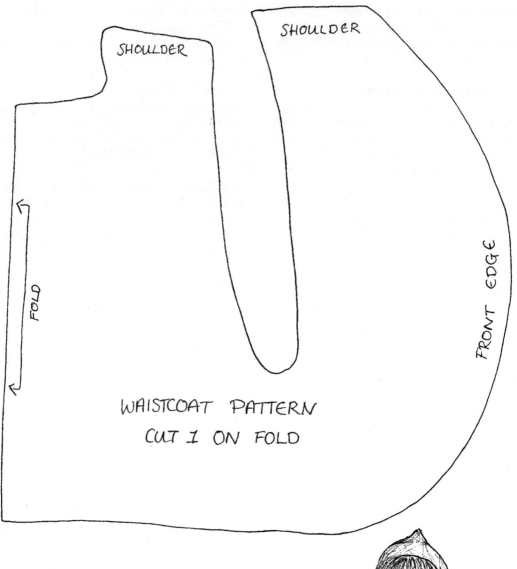

SHOULDER

SHOULDER

FOLD

FRONT EDGE

WAISTCOAT PATTERN
CUT 1 ON FOLD

Felt and leather need no further sewing. Other fabrics, which may fray, must have all the raw edges at arm holes and outside turned under and sewn down. You can do this using a running stitch with embroidery thread in a contrasting colour.

Extra embroidery can be sewn to the waistcoat fronts and backs to add more colour and interest.

Skirt
Materials
Thin cotton 5″ x 15″ (20cm x 35cm)
½″ (1cm) elastic - 6″ (15cm) long
Sewing thread

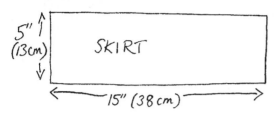

Method
1. With right sides together machine a seam ½″ (1cm) from the edge joining the short sides of the fabric together.

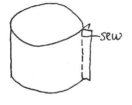

2. On one long edge (bottom of skirt) turn under ½″ (1cm) to wrong side and machine sew. This is the hem.

3. On the other long side turn over ¼″ (0.5cm) and then 1″ (2.5cm), on the wrong side and machine all round leaving a 1″ (2.5cm) gap at centre back.

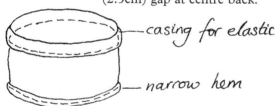

4. Fasten a safety pin on one end of the elastic and pull through the casing you have made. Remove the pin and knot the ends of the elastic together. Try on the doll and shorten elastic if necessary. Sew the opening closed with a few stitches.

Add a lace trim to the hem for extra prettiness.

Dress
Materials
Thin cotton 7″ x 20″ (17.5 x 50cm)
½yd (50cm) narrow ribbon in matching colour
Lace trim 20″ (50cm) long
Sewing cotton to match

Method
1. Cut slits for armholes as shown in the diagram.

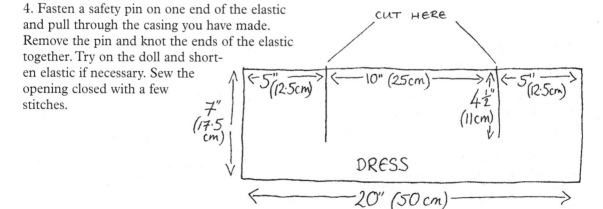

2. Neaten and turn under all the raw edges except the top (neck edge). The quickest way to do this is to zigzag all the edges and then turn under ¹/₂″ (1cm) all round. Otherwise, turn ³/₈″ (0.5cm) under twice and machine around or hem the raw edges by hand.

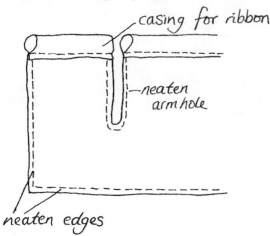

3. Sew on a lace trim to the bottom of the dress.

4. At top edges turn under first ³/₈″ (0.5cm) and then ³/₄″ (1.5cm) to form a casing for the ribbon; make this casing across all three parts of the top piece.

5. Using a safety pin, thread the ribbon through the top edge. Arrange so an equal length of ribbon extends at each side.

6. Take a few running stitches through the ribbon and fabric at the front so the ribbon cannot be pulled out accidentally. Put the dress on the doll and pull up the ribbon at neck to fit the doll and tie in a bow at the back.

Knitted or crocheted garments

No specific instructions are given, as these are simply rectangles worked to the sizes given. Use yarn, needles and crochet hooks as necessary to get the shapes drawn below. An exact fit is unnecessary as the work will stretch easily.

Jerkin

Stripes in lots of different colours are very cheerful and easy to work.

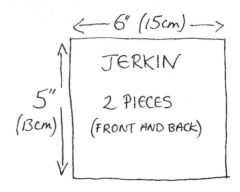

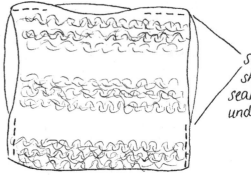

Waistcoat (Vest)

Sew the back to the fronts at the shoulders and
at the side seam. Sew a twisted or plaited cord
at the top to tie.

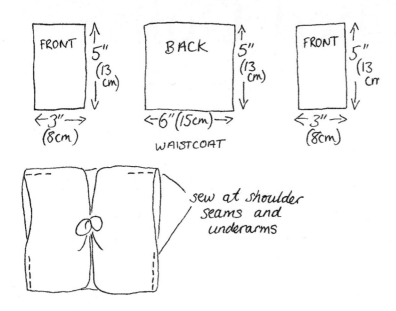

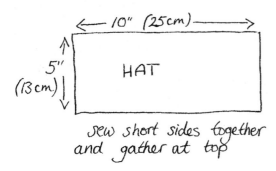

sew at shoulder
seams and
underarms

Hat (for dolls with hair)

Sew the two short sides together to make a
tube and then sew a line of running stitches
along one long edge.

sew short sides together
and gather at top

Draw the stitched edges together and sew all of
the top edges together. Turn
so seams are hidden. A
pom-pom or tassel can
be added if desired.

Chapter 5

Limbed Dolls

Limbed dolls are those made entirely from skin-coloured knit fabric. They can be made in many sizes – small enough to carry round in a pocket or large enough to wear first size baby clothes – they can be dressed in different outfits and will give immense pleasure to their owners over many years.

There is something very special about making a doll for one particular child. It takes time, thought and effort to create this wonderful gift, all of which is reflected in the completed project. Every doll made will be individual, with its own character. When I hold workshops with ten or twelve aspiring dollmakers I am amazed at how different each doll becomes. We all start with the same materials and work from the same instructions, yet each creation is unique. There is often more than a passing resemblance to one's own child. This is not only in the doll's colouring, which may have been consciously imitated, but also on some deeper level. I do not suggest that you try to model the doll's structure on that of its intended owner, only that you keep him or her in your mind as you work.

One mother came to me somewhat reluctantly, saying she thought she 'ought' to make a doll for her son's birthday even though 'he only plays with cars and guns'. We worked together and made a large doll with an untidy head of brown hair and a lopsided grin. The mother had tried resewing the mouth several times but it always slanted to one side. I was concerned that there would be an ugly mark made by the repeated stitching so we decided to leave the mouth as it was. The doll was kitted out with trousers and jacket in sand-coloured fabric, given a floppy hat and an amazing backpack filled with tiny treasures – including a small compass, penknife, a miniature map (reduced on a colour photocopier), a tiny torch and a doll-sized sleeping bag.

On the evening before the birthday the gift was wrapped and put on Roger's bedside table. When his mother came in to wake him neither doll nor child were to be seen. They were both under the bed, for as Roger said 'He's an explorer and so am I'. Later that day Roger's mother asked what he liked best about his new friend and Roger said 'I like the way I know he's happy to smile and talk to me, because his mouth is all ready for moving, he's just thinking what to say next.' Sometimes mistakes can be your biggest successes!

I feel that a child should not have a large number of dolls. Just as in a family every member needs their own space – physically and emotionally – so each doll needs to be given room in the heart. Every child should have one special doll which is of a good size, perhaps with a colouring similar to their own, and then one or two others to keep it company and provide opportunities for imaginative play.

One of the ways a child makes sense of the world around them is by copying the actions and mannerisms of those around them. The more central an adult is to their life the more likely they are to try and copy them. So much of a child's play is focused on the home, and later, kindergarten or preschool. The doll takes on the role of the child whilst the child can become an all-knowing parent or teacher. The child learns and 'makes sense' of the world about them by repeating and enlarging on activities that occur regularly.

I always knew exactly what had happened during my daughter's time at kindergarten because she would come home at lunch time and spend the afternoon recreating her morning. She would group all her dolls and soft toys in front of her and make them take the part of the other children. They each had their own characters; a golden-haired doll was always the naughty one that had to be taken aside and talked firmly to, another was the shy new boy who stood by himself at the edge of the group and had to be coaxed to join in, another wanted to spend her time sitting on teacher's lap and so on. An adult would interpret this as role playing, trying out different scenarios, experimenting with possible outcomes but for a child it is 'just play'.

Sometimes adult actions are incomprehensible to a child and working them through with a doll as their patient and unquestioning companion is vital. Even obvious and everyday tasks seem strange to a young child. For instance, why do people gather up all the clothes they were quite happy to wear the previous day, stuff them through an open window or door , close the window and press a few knobs, before leaving the object alone to make funny noises. Much later we return and get wet clothes out which then have to be dried before being put back in the cupboard and worn again.

It's much easier for a child to understand the process of cleaning and washing if they can take part and see the water getting dirty as they swish the clothes around and smell how clean and fresh line-dried clothes really are.

Imitation and repetition are key activities for under sevens and having their own special friend to help them with these activities is very important.

Do not think that because a doll is not played with constantly it is not loved or needed. A friend made a beautiful doll for Michael, her 10 year old

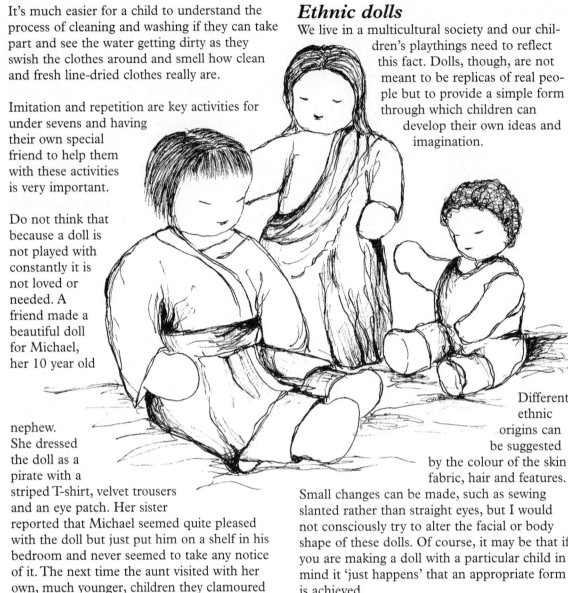

nephew. She dressed the doll as a pirate with a striped T-shirt, velvet trousers and an eye patch. Her sister reported that Michael seemed quite pleased with the doll but just put him on a shelf in his bedroom and never seemed to take any notice of it. The next time the aunt visited with her own, much younger, children they clamoured to play with the pirate doll. Their cousin agreed and when it was time to go the little ones didn't want to let the doll go. Michael's mother took him aside and suggested that the cousins could 'borrow' the pirate for a time. Michael considered but then shook his head: 'We talk every night before I go to sleep and I think he'd be lonely without me.' Michael's aunt had to promise to make another pirate doll for her own family and peace was restored.

Ethnic dolls

We live in a multicultural society and our children's playthings need to reflect this fact. Dolls, though, are not meant to be replicas of real people but to provide a simple form through which children can develop their own ideas and imagination.

Different ethnic origins can be suggested by the colour of the skin fabric, hair and features. Small changes can be made, such as sewing slanted rather than straight eyes, but I would not consciously try to alter the facial or body shape of these dolls. Of course, it may be that if you are making a doll with a particular child in mind it 'just happens' that an appropriate form is achieved.

Clothes are also important; observe – from life or from photos and books – and then design the right outfit for your doll. Keep the line of the garment simple but use different types and colours of fabrics to emphasise the origins intended for the doll. Some suggestions are given in the chapter on clothes but the simple shapes of the patterns make it easy to adapt to your own ideas.

Instructions

These instructions are for a 14 - 16″ (35 - 40cm) doll which is just right as a child's most important doll. It is substantial enough to dress and play with and can also be carried around easily.

You can choose between the traditional style doll with its arms and legs sewn onto the body or the jointed 'baby' style which has separate and moveable limbs. The traditional doll is best for the older child (6 years onwards) and will often develop a real character of its own, becoming a true best friend for its owner. The jointed type is easier to dress and undress and would suit a younger child. It is also nice to make and give as a second doll – perhaps when a new baby is expected in the family or just as a special present.

Jointed doll

Traditional doll

Proportions

The head is approximately a quarter of the total length of the doll. The remaining three-quarters is divided equally between the torso and the legs, with an extra amount for the feet. The correct length for the arms is for them to reach the groin when hanging loosely, and just meet when held above the head. Shorter arms indicate a baby doll, longer give an adult effect.

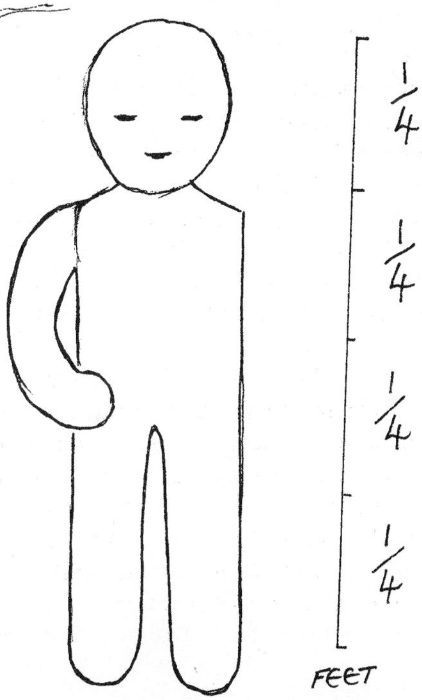

$\frac{1}{4}$

$\frac{1}{4}$

$\frac{1}{4}$

$\frac{1}{4}$

FEET

Stuffing

Use clean sheepswool. The wool should be carded or teased to remove any knots and should be light and fluffy.

Take small pieces of wool and push well down as you go. This takes longer but gives a more even finish. You can use a rounded stick or piece of dowel to help get the stuffing in the right place but be very careful not to over-stretch or break the cotton knit fabric.

Always stuff both parts of a 'pair', i.e. arms or legs, at the same time and check they end up the same size and shape! Cotton knit is very stretchy and can easily be forced into very odd shapes; you must mould it with your hands so that natural looking limbs and body shapes are made.

The aim is to achieve a smooth, firm feel, not too rigid but dense enough to withstand wear and tear. Wool will pack down slightly with time so always add one more piece after you are satisfied with the feel.

Materials for a 14 - 16" (35 - 40cm) doll

Circle of white cotton knit 12" (30cm) diameter
27" (70cm) of skin-coloured cotton knit (36" [100cm] wide)
11b (500gm) washed and carded sheepswool
Crochet cotton or other thick thread
Sewing thread to match (a) body fabric
                          (b) hair colour
Embroidery thread for features
2oz (50gm) knitting wool and 1oz (25gm) mohair (optional) for hair
Glass-headed pins

N.B. The weights of sheepswool given are for guidance only; please read the information about fleece in the chapter on General Techniques.

To make the head

1. Take 4oz (100gm) of the sheepswool and divide it into thirds. Put two thirds aside, this will be used to make the inner core of the head.

2. Divide the remaining one third (approx. 1¼oz or 30gm) into two pieces and lay one piece over the other at right angles to make a cross.

3. Mould the remaining two thirds of the wool (approx. 2¾oz or 70gm) into a rough ball of 3" (8cm) diameter. This should be quite hard and firm. Place in the centre of the sheepswool cross and bring the 'arms' of the cross down and around the inner ball. There will be some wool hanging down below the main ball; this forms the neck. Grasp this neck and place the whole inner head in the centre of the white cotton knit circle. Do not let go of the wool or you will have to start this part all over again.

4. Gather the cotton knit fabric around the wool head, drawing the fabric around so as to cover all the wool. Some of the fabric should hang below the wool. Now transfer your grip so you are still holding onto the neck but include the white fabric in your hand. Keep a tight hold.

tie at neck

Take a length of crochet cotton (about 20" [50cm]) and wrap tightly twice around the neck and tie securely. This can be difficult to manage one-handed at first but does get easier with practice. You can always enlist a friend to be your 'third hand' if necessary.

5. Look carefully at the shape and size of the head. Check it is the right size for the doll you are making. It should be 4″ (10cm) high from neck to top of head and 14 - 15″ (35 - 38cm) round the widest part (or circumference) for a 16″ (40cm) doll. Decide where you want the front or face to be. Look for a nice chin shape, not too flat, nor with too many gathers or pleats in the material. You can pummel and push the head to get a better shape if necessary, but don't be too rough or you may lose the basic round shape.

6. Cut a piece of crochet thread (or thick thread) at least 30″ (75cm) long and tie *eyeline* round the head to mark the eyeline. To do this hold the thread 4″ (10cm) from one end and tie around the head about half way down, start at the side of the head where the ear would be, and wrap the thread twice round the head. Pull the thread tight so that there is a clear indentation and tie the two ends firmly together at the side of the head. You now have one long and one short length of thread hanging down.

7. Take the longer thread and pass over the top of the head (1) and right down to the centre of the neck at the front of the head. This thread crosses the eyeline string at the side (where the other ear would be) and goes under the chin.

FRONT OF HEAD

FRONT VIEW

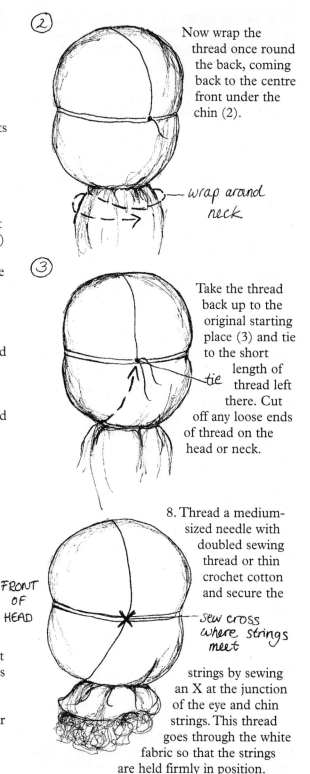

② Now wrap the thread once round the back, coming back to the centre front under the chin (2).

— *wrap around neck*

③ Take the thread back up to the original starting place (3) and tie to the short length of thread left there. Cut off any loose ends of thread on the head or neck.

— *tie*

8. Thread a medium-sized needle with doubled sewing thread or thin crochet cotton and secure the *sew cross where strings meet* strings by sewing an X at the junction of the eye and chin strings. This thread goes through the white fabric so that the strings are held firmly in position.

9. Gently pull the string at the back of the head down to meet the neck string. This can sometimes be a little difficult if the string is very tight, in which case you can help the string to move by pushing the back of the neck and compressing the sheepswool so that it slips under the string.

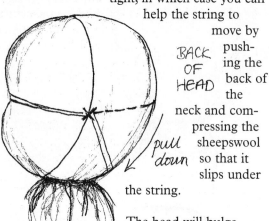

BACK OF HEAD

pull down

The head will bulge between these lower back and chin strings, giving a lumpy look to the doll. To remove this sew, with doubled sewing thread, across the bulge from one thick thread to another. Take a small stitch into the white fabric at each side. The purpose of this is to flatten the lump, not to draw the threads together, so do not make the criss-cross thread too tight. You now have a nicely shaped (and finished) inner head.

sew across

of the back of the head and finishing at the fold at the centre front. Continue the line for 4″ (10cm) below the neck, you will use this to make a neat muff, or shoulder pad, for the doll.

Remove the head and cut out the head covering, leaving an extra ¹/₂″ (1cm) for a seam allowance.

FOLD

clip

2. Machine stitch on the line you have marked. Clip at the curve of the neck, snip with sharp scissors up to (but not over) the line of stitching. Turn the head cover the right way round and place over the head with the seam at centre back. You may need to gently stretch and pull the fabric cover down to get it smooth and neat. When you have the head cover in position then tie, with crochet cotton, round the neck.

tie at neck

Head covering

1. Place the inner head on a doubled piece of skin-coloured cotton knit fabric – the front of the face is along the fold. Make sure that the grain (or lines) of the fabric go from the top to the bottom of the head, the most 'give' or stretch lies across the doll's face. Draw the shape of the head onto the cotton knit, following the curves

3. Check the top of the head, the seam should finish neatly at the centre front where the hair will cover it. If the end of the seam sticks up then tuck this under and inside the head cover, sewing down with a few stitches.

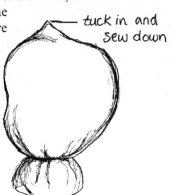

tuck in and Sew down

4. Make a shoulder pad or muff with the wool and white fabric from below the neck. It may be necessary to add a little more wool to ensure there is a small but solid base to the head. It is important for this pad to be firm and for it to incorporate the wool that comes down out of the head because this is what keeps the neck solid and stops the head from wobbling.

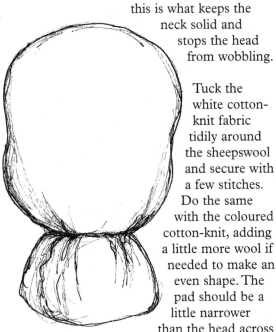

Tuck the white cotton-knit fabric tidily around the sheepswool and secure with a few stitches. Do the same with the coloured cotton-knit, adding a little more wool if needed to make an even shape. The pad should be a little narrower than the head across the shoulders and about half this width from front to back.

Features

1. Mark the position of the eyes and mouth with glass-headed pins. Use two of the same colour for the eyes and a different colour for the mouth. Place the eyes on the eyestring and the mouth centrally below them, forming a triangular shape. Check the spacing is even and keep moving the pins until you are satisfied. This is the single most important part of the doll, and it is worth taking time to get it right. The distance between the eyes and the mouth should be equal and not too close together, but it is more important that the features look balanced rather than being mathematically precise. Use your own judgement to achieve a pleasing result.

2. **Eyes**
Thread a long needle with six strands of embroidery thread in an appropriate colour and fasten securely at the side of the head where it will be hidden by the hair.

Bring the needle through the head and come out slightly to one side of the pin marking one of the eyes. Take a straight stitch over the site of the pin – do not make the eye too small. Make 1 or 2 more stitches over the original one, in exactly the same place, then take the needle through the head to the side or back and fasten securely. Repeat for the other eye taking care to match the position and size of the first eye.

3. **Mouth**
The colour of the mouth should be of a similar intensity to the eyes and also a colour which will complement the eyes and the hair colour. A coral shade often looks more natural than bright pink or red.

Thread a long needle and fasten at side of head as for the eyes and bring through the head to one side of the mouth pin. The mouth consists of two stitches, one long, one short. The longer *mouth* stitch is about one and a half times the length of the eye and

goes across the site of the pin marking the mouth. The shorter stitch is half the length of the first and is placed centrally below it. Fasten at the back as for the eyes.

Mistakes

If you need to unpick these stitches, be very careful not to cut into or snag the fabric as it will ladder or hole easily. Try to cut the thread at the back and pull out from the rear of the head. Marks from needles can be lessened by rubbing with a damp finger.

Do not rework features more than once – it makes too much mess – remember a little unevenness adds character! If you are very unsure about the actual length of stitches etc. then mark lightly with a pencil before sewing.

The head is now finished; it can be used for either the traditional or jointed bodies.

Alternative way to make the inner head

The instructions above explain how to make an inner head from a circle of fabric. It is also possible to use tubular bandage or a sewn tube, as described for making the inner heads of soft dolls. Some people find this easier at first, but the finished shape is not so pleasing, being less rounded at the back of the head. New dollmakers have a tendency to make the whole head too long and narrow when starting from a tube.

HEAD FROM TUBE

HEAD FROM CIRCLE

Tubing is also less versatile. Once you have mastered the art of making the inner head from a flat piece of material then any size head can be made quite easily. The main exception is when making a very large doll with a head height of 6″ (15cm) or more, then the quantity of fleece and size of cotton circle becomes unwieldy and it is simpler to use a piece of tubing.

Making the inner head from a tube

Prepare the tube by tying and turning as for the sack doll.

Mould the head from sheepswool as described above (instructions #1, 2 and 3). Place the fleece ball inside the tubing. Add more stuffing as necessary to fill the tube.

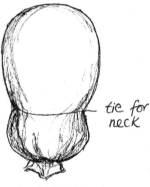

Tie, with strong thread, at the bottom and again for the neck. See the chapter on soft dolls for more detailed instructions.

tie for neck

The lower portion of the inner head now becomes the muff. It needs to be shortened and to have some extra stitches taken across its width to make a neat shape for the shoulders.

Continue from #6 as for the head made from a circle.

Note: to make a head for a 16 - 18″ (40 - 45cm) doll you need tubing 2½ - 3″ (16 - 18cm) wide and 14″ (35cm) long.

Traditional limbed doll

These measurements apply to a
doll with a 4″ (10cm) head
and a finished height of
16″ (40cm).

A full size pattern is
given for this size doll
on pages 86 and 87.
The pattern does
not include any
seam allowances. I
find the easiest way
to get an accurate shape
on the material is to
draw round the actual
size pattern and then
cut out 1cm away from
the line drawn. You can
then sew on the line you
have marked.

Body

1. Using the pattern given cut out the body and
arms (legs are cut with the body). Make sure
you cut out on a double piece of cotton knit
fabric and check that the grain (or lines) of the
fabric go down the length of the body and
down the arms. The most stretch goes across
the body and arms.

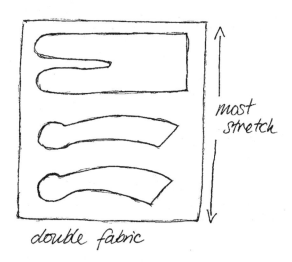

double fabric

most stretch

2. Sew the body and arms by machine, using a
small zigzag or other stretch stitch. Remember
to leave 2″ (5cm) unsewn at the top of the
body piece so that the arms can be sewn in
later.

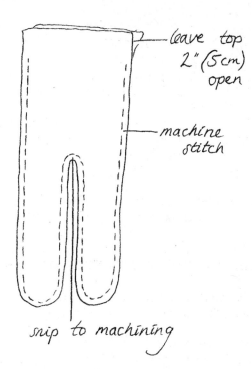

leave top
2″ (5cm)
open

machine
stitch

snip to machining

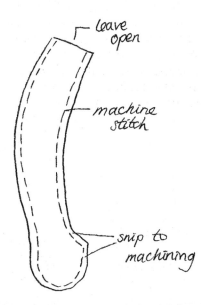

leave
open

machine
stitch

snip to
machining

These pattern pieces have been cut in half because they go across two pages. They have to be joined at the dotted line when you trace them.

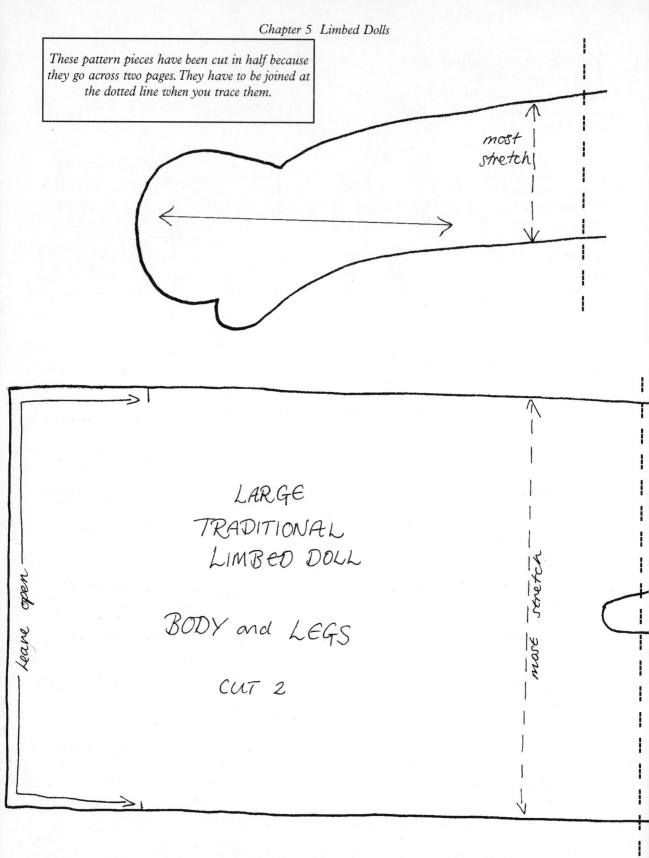

most stretch

LARGE
TRADITIONAL
LIMBED DOLL

BODY and LEGS

CUT 2

leave open

more stretch

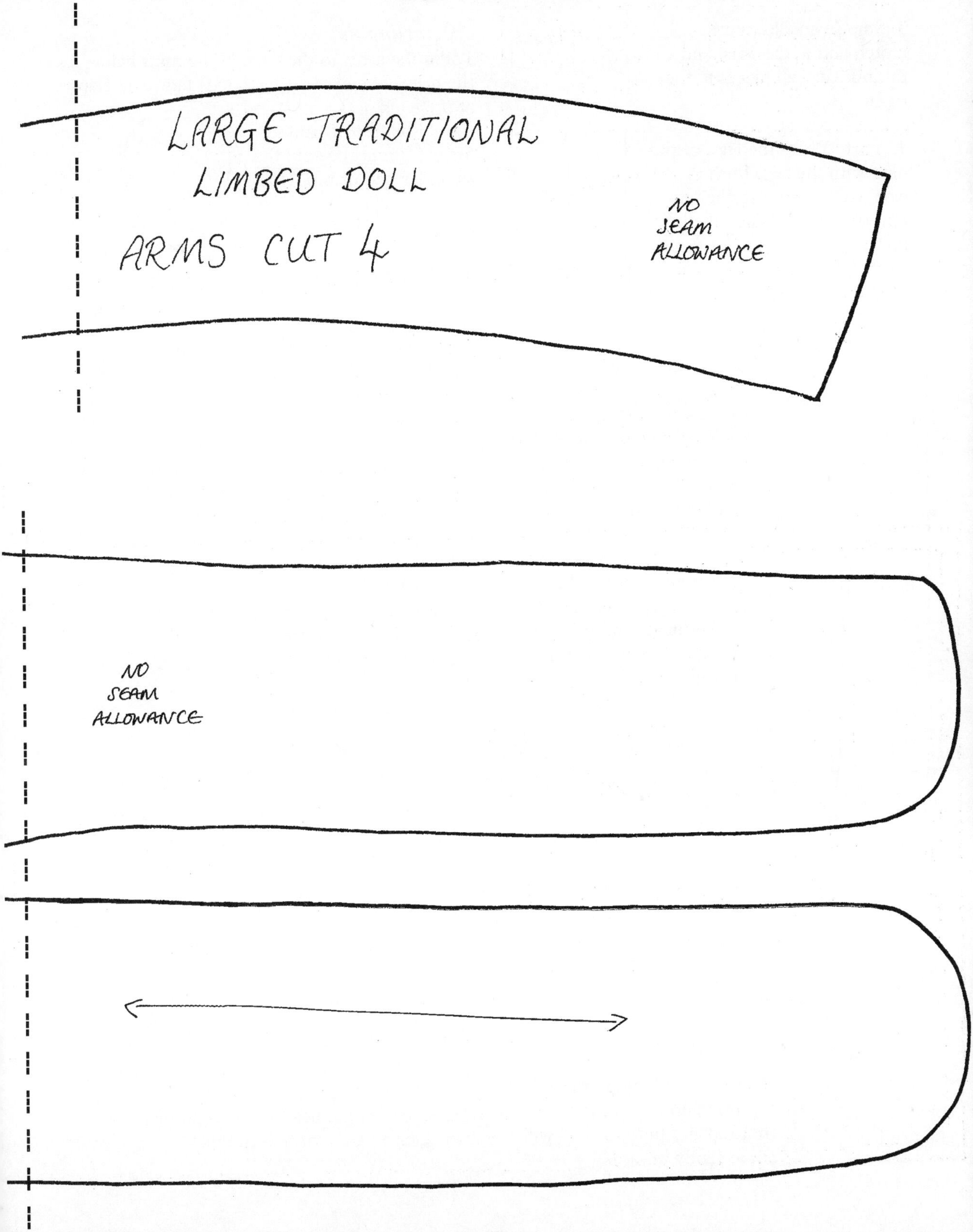

LARGE TRADITIONAL
LIMBED DOLL

ARMS CUT 4

NO
SEAM
ALLOWANCE

NO
SEAM
ALLOWANCE

3. Snip seam allowance at crotch and at the wrist and thumb. Turn all pieces to the right side.

4. Start to stuff the legs, beginning with the feet. Push the wool well down into the bottom of the legs. When the first inch or so (2 or 3cm) is firmly stuffed place a pin across to keep the stuffing for the feet separate from that in the legs.

5. Continue stuffing the legs until you reach the groin, put another pin at the top of each leg. These pins need to be at an angle of 45 degrees, so that the doll will bend naturally and be able to sit.

6. Now stuff the torso up to the opening left for the arms. The doll needs to be stuffed firmly and this will take about ¹/₂lb (250gm) of sheepswool.

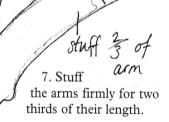

stuff ⅔ of arm

7. Stuff the arms firmly for two thirds of their length.

shoulder

arm

seam

The seam goes along the centre front and back of the arm (not top and bottom) and will curve gently inwards.

Assembling the doll

1. Pin the arms to the back of the muff below the head. The excess (unstuffed) fabric overlaps at the back of the muff and should be free of stuffing for ¹/₂″ (1cm) beyond the shoulder pad or muff.

2. Insert muff and arms into the top of the body, pin the fabric neatly around neck and across the top of the muff, thus forming the shoulders.

pin arms to muff

3. Hold up the doll and check the length of the arms. The arms should hang down as far as the top of the legs and just meet above the head. When you are satisfied that the proportions are right then unpin and remove the head and arms from the body. Sew arms securely to muff, making sure that they are free of stuffing for a little way beyond the shoulder pad.

shoulder

arm

sew by hand

This ensures they will hang down rather than sticking out stiffly from the shoulder.

4. Put the arms back into body and pin in place again. Sew neatly around the neck, attempting to avoid the pins which will try to stick into your fingers! It's easiest to sew round twice, once to secure the head in the right place and then again to get a neat even finish.

5. Sew neatly along the top of the shoulders and around the arms. There should be no stuffing at the point where the arms meet the shoulders.

6. Remove the pin from one side of the groin and, with a double thread, sew across the top of the leg using a stab stitch. This line of stitches needs to be sewn diagonally to the crotch. Repeat for the other side.

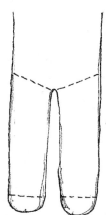

sew crotch and feet

7. Remove the pin from one foot and sew across, using a stab stitch. Repeat for the other side. If you wish, the foot may be sewn again so that it is fixed at right angles to the leg.

foot

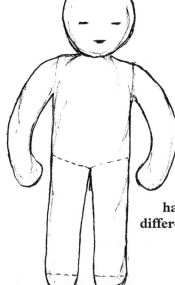

Hair – refer to Chapter 2 on hair for lots of different ideas.

Jointed doll

The full size pattern which is given is suitable for a doll with a 4″ (10cm) head. No allowance has been made for seams; you need to add 1cm all round.

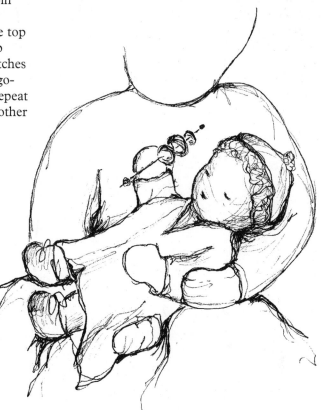

1. Trace the patterns on the following pages for the large jointed doll. Cut out all the pattern pieces, making sure the grain of the fabric runs down the limbs and body and the greatest stretch goes across the pieces.

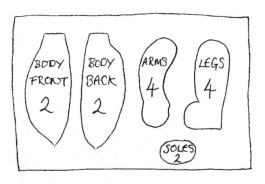

BODY FRONT 2

BODY BACK 2

ARMS 4

LEGS 4

SOLES 2

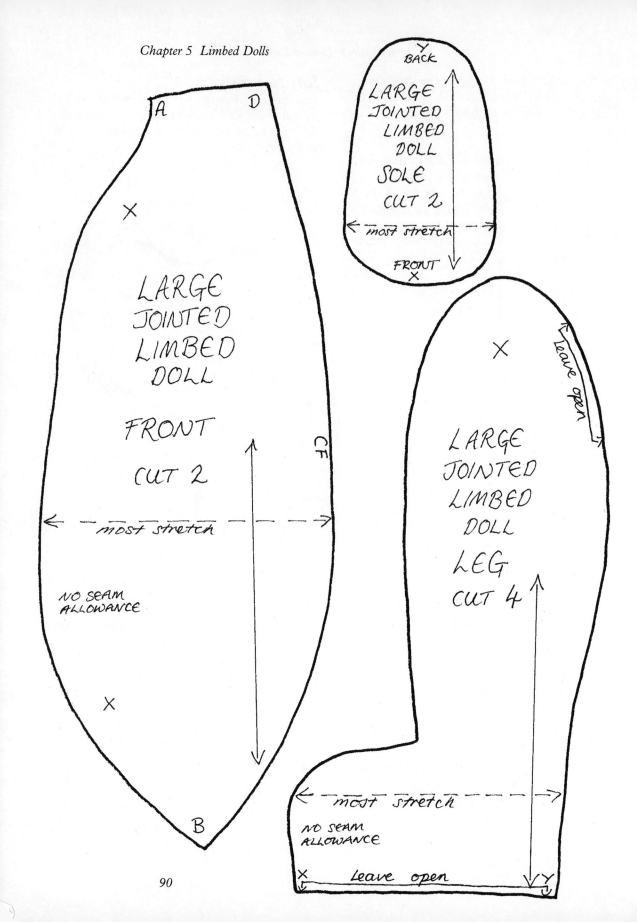

Y
BACK

LARGE
JOINTED
LIMBED
DOLL
SOLE
CUT 2

most stretch

FRONT
X

A   D

×

LARGE
JOINTED
LIMBED
DOLL

FRONT

CUT 2

CF

most stretch

NO SEAM
ALLOWANCE

×

B

leave open

×

LARGE
JOINTED
LIMBED
DOLL
LEG
CUT 4

most stretch

NO SEAM
ALLOWANCE

X   leave open   Y

90

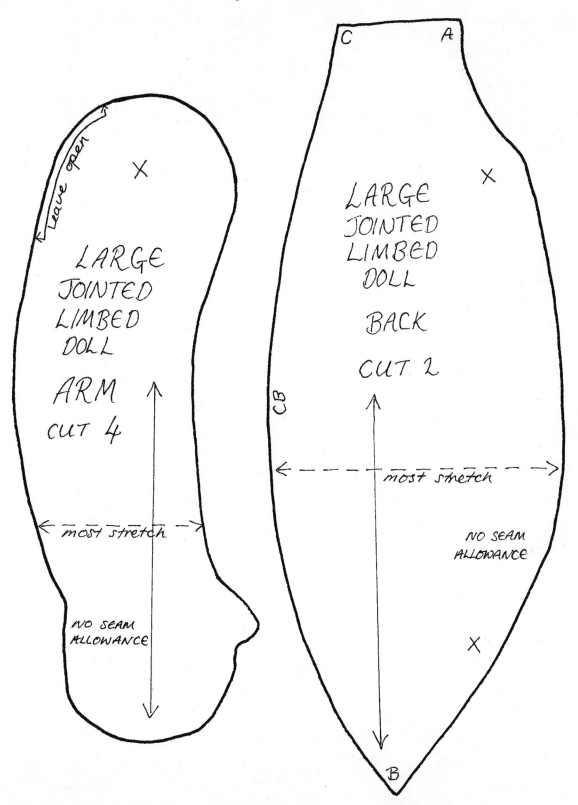

Leave open

LARGE JOINTED LIMBED DOLL

ARM

CUT 4

most stretch

NO SEAM ALLOWANCE

C   A

LARGE JOINTED LIMBED DOLL

BACK

CUT 2

CB

most stretch

NO SEAM ALLOWANCE

B

2. Check you have all the necessary pieces:
    2 front body pieces
    2 back body pieces
    4 arms
    4 legs
    2 soles
Make sure you can identify the back and front body pieces – either make a faint pencil mark or sew a coloured thread to the top of the back pieces.

3. Assembly

Machine sew the centre front and centre back seams of the body (i.e. C to B and D to B) and then the side seams from neck edge to crotch and back to neck (A to B to A). You now have a pear shaped bag with an opening at the top or neck edge. Stuff firmly.

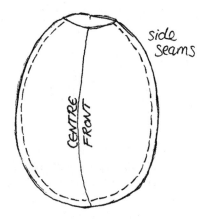

4. Sew arms and legs together in pairs, leaving openings as shown. Do not forget to leave two openings on the legs, one for the insertion of the soles and the other for stuffing.

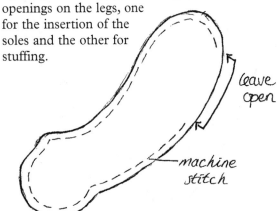

Pin, tack and sew the sole into bottom of leg. This can be quite tricky, so you may find it easier to sew the sole by hand, using small back stitches.

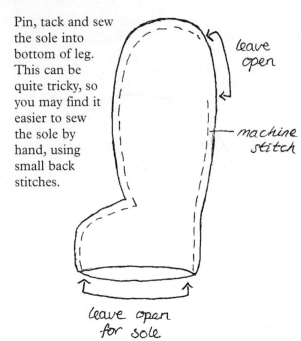

5. Snip to the seam allowance, but NOT across the stitches at the ankles and hands. Turn all pieces to the right side, with all the seams inside, stuff firmly. Slip-stitch the openings in arms and legs.

6. Place muff of head inside body. Check the stuffing fits smoothly around the muff and adjust as necessary. Make sure the back and front of the body are correctly positioned with seams at centre and side. Turn raw edges of fabric in around the neck, stitch neatly and securely.

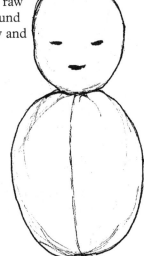

7. Position arms on body, using the markings on the pattern as a guide. Thread a long needle with a double crochet cotton thread. Take needle and thread from one arm, through the body and through the second arm. Cut the thread leaving 6″ (15cm) hanging down each side. Bring the double thread back through the arm, body, arm sequence about 1/2″ (1cm) from the first thread, and leaving 6″ (15cm) at each side. Knot the four threads firmly together on one side. Then pull threads tightly and tie at other side.

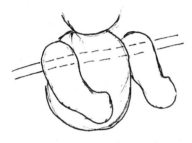

Repeat for the legs.

Check the legs are in the correct place by putting the doll in a sitting position. The legs should now be supporting the doll and at a 90 degree (right angle) to the body, with their lower edge flush with the ground. The arms are placed about midway between the top of the legs and the neck. Do not place too high or the doll's neck will disappear.

The thread needs to be as tight as possible because over a period of time it will stretch, loosening the joint. When that happens the thread can either be cut and retied, if there is enough yarn, or completely rethreaded. A synthetic yarn does not stretch in the same way but, as it is tougher than the cotton knit, may well work through the fabric of the limbs leaving an unsightly hole.

Hair – refer to Chapter 2 on hair for lots of different ideas.

Smaller dolls

Full-sized patterns for traditional and jointed bodies for **medium** and **small** dolls are given. Trace off the pieces needed for the doll you want to make.

The heads are best constructed using the smaller sizes of circles listed here, but the patterns are of such a size that the inner head made for the sack doll can be used for the medium doll and the inner head for the baggy doll for the small doll. The heads need to be fully shaped – that is with chin strings and sewn shapings at the neck – as for the large doll.

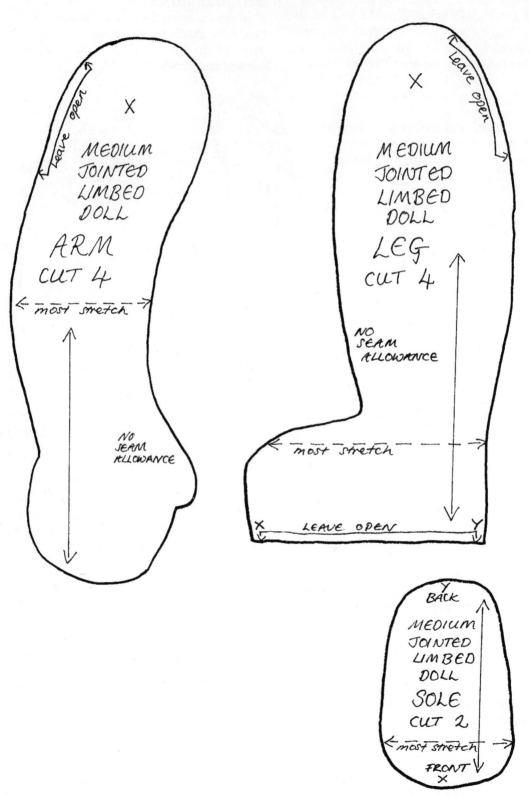

MEDIUM
JOINTED
LIMBED
DOLL

ARM
CUT 4

Leave open

X

most stretch

NO
SEAM
ALLOWANCE

MEDIUM
JOINTED
LIMBED
DOLL

LEG
CUT 4

Leave open

X

NO
SEAM
ALLOWANCE

most stretch

LEAVE OPEN

BACK
X

MEDIUM
JOINTED
LIMBED
DOLL

SOLE
CUT 2

most stretch

FRONT
X

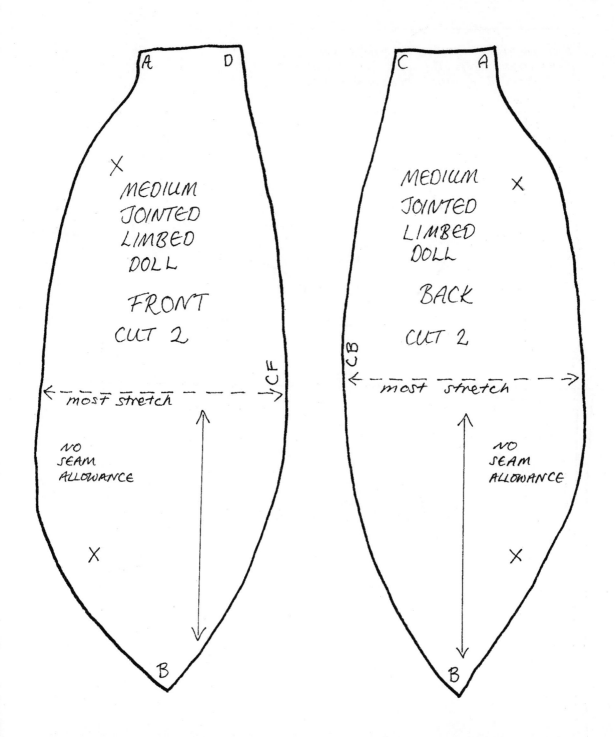

A   D

MEDIUM
JOINTED
LIMBED
DOLL

FRONT

CUT 2

← most stretch →   CF

NO
SEAM
ALLOWANCE

X

B

C   A

MEDIUM
JOINTED
LIMBED
DOLL

BACK

CUT 2

CB ← most stretch →

NO
SEAM
ALLOWANCE

X

B

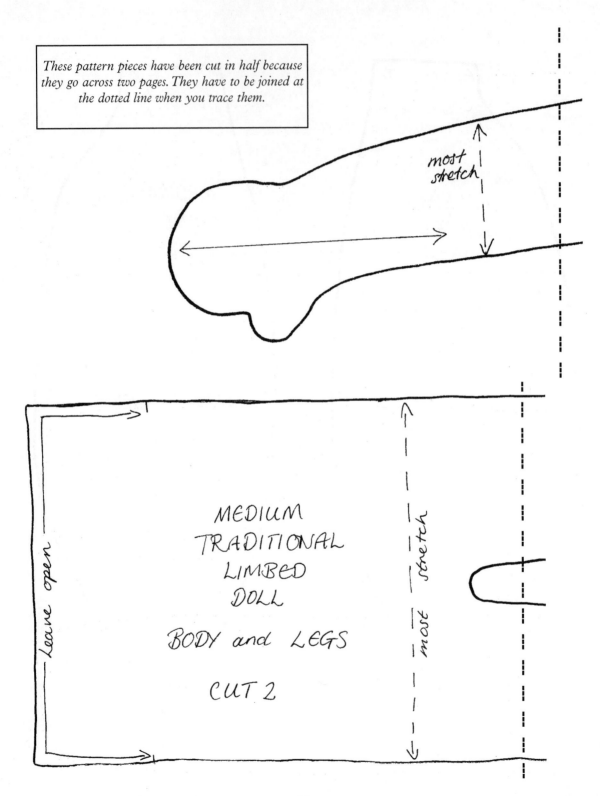

These pattern pieces have been cut in half because they go across two pages. They have to be joined at the dotted line when you trace them.

most stretch

MEDIUM
TRADITIONAL
LIMBED
DOLL

BODY and LEGS

CUT 2

Leave open

most stretch

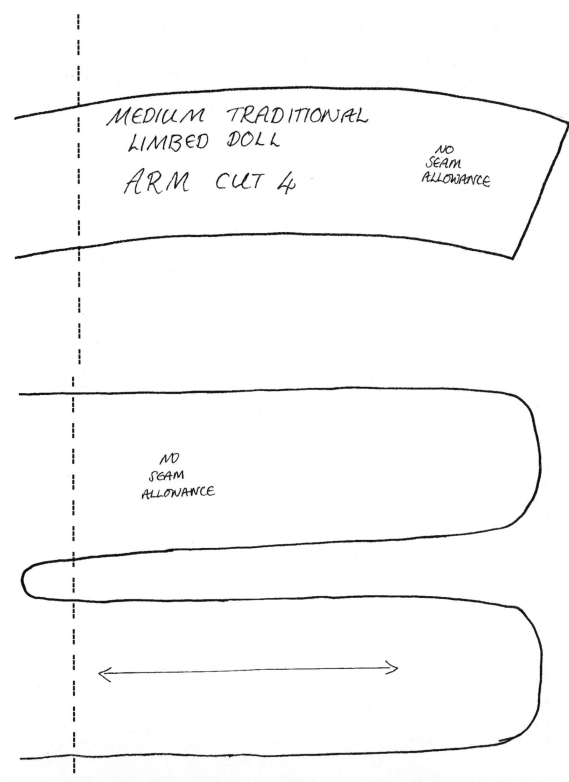

MEDIUM TRADITIONAL
LIMBED DOLL

ARM CUT 4

NO
SEAM
ALLOWANCE

NO
SEAM
ALLOWANCE

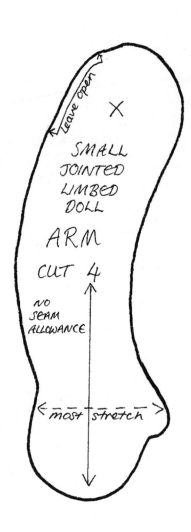

Leave open

X

SMALL
JOINTED
LIMBED
DOLL

ARM

CUT 4

NO
SEAM
ALLOWANCE

← most stretch →

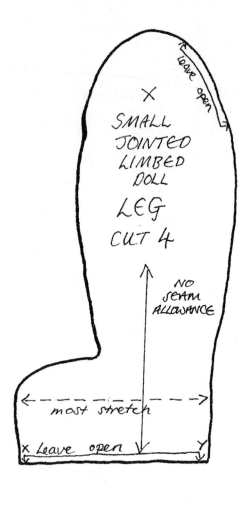

Leave open

X

SMALL
JOINTED
LIMBED
DOLL

LEG

CUT 4

NO
SEAM
ALLOWANCE

← most stretch →

X Leave open

Y
BACK

SMALL
JOINTED
LIMBED
DOLL
SOLE
CUT 2

← most stretch →

FRONT
X

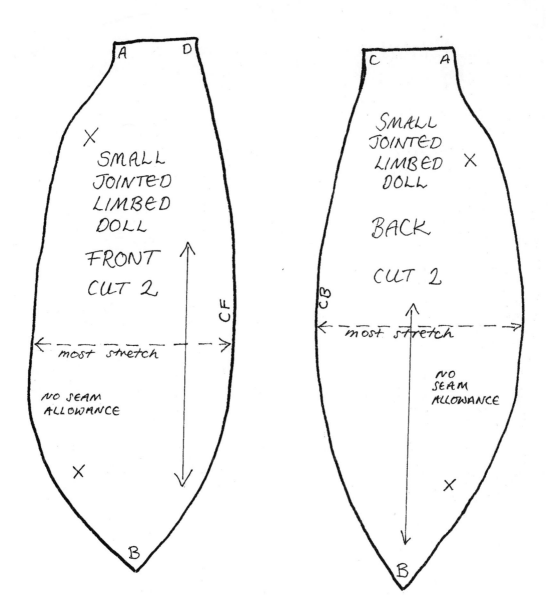

A   D

X

SMALL
JOINTED
LIMBED
DOLL

FRONT
CUT 2

CF

← most stretch →

NO SEAM
ALLOWANCE

X

B

C   A

SMALL
JOINTED
LIMBED
DOLL

BACK

CUT 2

CB

← most stretch →

NO
SEAM
ALLOWANCE

X

B

Leave open

Leave open

Leave open

SMALL
TRADITIONAL
LIMBED DOLL

BODY and
LEGS

CUT 2

most stretch

NO
SEAM
ALLOWANCE

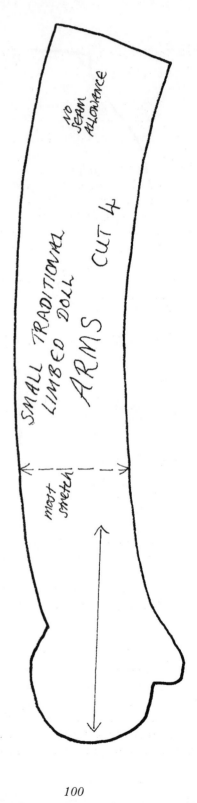

no
seam
allowance

SMALL TRADITIONAL
LIMBED DOLL
ARMS   CUT 4

most stretch

Follow the basic instructions for the large doll (16″ or 40cm) with the following adjustments.

Medium doll (12″ or 30cm)

Materials
10″ (25cm) circle of white cotton knit
20″ (50 cm) of skin coloured cotton knit
11oz (300gm) washed and carded sheepswool
Other materials are as for the large doll.

Making the doll
Divide the sheepswool and use 3oz (85gm) for making the head and the remaining 8oz (215gm) for stuffing the body.
The final measurements for the head are 3″ (8cm) high and 11″ (28cm) circumference.

Follow the instructions for either the traditional or the jointed doll using the pattern for the medium doll.

Small doll (9″ or 23cm)

Materials
8″ (20cm) circle of white cotton knit
15″ (40 cm) of skin-coloured cotton knit
8oz (250gm) washed and carded sheepswool
Other materials are as for the large doll.

Making the doll
Divide the sheepswool and use 2oz (50gm) for making the head and the remaining 6oz (150gm) for stuffing the body.

The final measurements for the head are 2½″ (7.5cm) high and 9″ (23cm) circumference.

Follow the instructions for either the traditional or the jointed doll using the pattern for the small doll.

Larger dolls
I have not provided detailed instructions and patterns for dolls larger than 16″ (40cm) in this book because, while the construction, techniques etc., are the same as for smaller dolls, they do require a greater level of skill. Once you have made some of the other dolls in this book

you will have no difficulty in adapting the patterns to make any size of doll.

Altering the pattern
Traditional style dolls can be made larger (or smaller) by first making the appropriate size head and then cutting the body pattern accordingly.

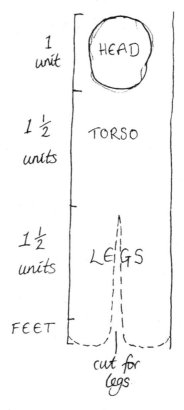

The head is taken as one unit, the torso (shoulder to crotch) equals one and a half, and the legs a further one and a half units, plus a small amount for the feet. Thus if the head measures 6″ (15cm), the torso will measure 9″ (23cm) and the legs 9″ (23cm), and the finished doll is 24″ (60cm).

The width of the doll's body is just a little wider than the head itself, a small amount is cut off to separate the legs.

Cut the arms from the closest size pattern drawn in this chapter, but make the width equal to the width of the legs.

The **jointed doll** patterns are more difficult to enlarge or reduce. You can redraw them free-hand to the size required; this works well if the finished doll is to be quite close in size to those shown here. If there is a greater change needed the patterns will have to be altered mechanically. One way is to draw a grid onto tracing paper, place over the pattern and transfer the shape, square by square, to a grid of larger (or smaller) squares.

The easiest method, however, is to take the patterns to a photocopy shop and ask to have them enlarged or reduced as required. An easy guide to calculating the percentage increase or decrease needed is to divide the original pattern size into the desired doll size. Thus to increase the pattern for a 16″ (40cm) doll to make one measuring 21″ (52.5cm), divide 16 into 21 (40 into 52.5) to get 1.31. Set the copier to 131%. To decrease the pattern for a 16″ (40cm) doll to make one measuring 13″ (32.5cm), divide 16 into 13 (40 into 32.5) to get 81. Set the copier to 81%.

The head height for the jointed dolls is about half the height of the body, but this is only a rough guide. I suggest that you make up the body and limbs of the doll, pin the arms and legs in place temporarily, and adjust the size of the inner head until it looks right when placed in position. The proportion of head to finished height of doll remains the same – the head is one fourth of the total length.

Making the doll
It is better to make the heads for large dolls from tubular bandage (or a sewn tube). Read the earlier section in this chapter entitled 'Alternative way to make the inner head'.

Dolls larger than 16 - 18″ (40 - 45cm) need to be made from a double thickness of fabric. Single fabric is not strong enough to cope with the larger areas of skin and greater weight of stuffing needed. Cut all the necessary parts, including the head cover, from double material. Treat the two thicknesses as if they were one, so

for the limbs of a jointed doll you will be sewing through four layers of fabric, and turning to have double fabric on each side of the limb.

A heavier weight cotton knit with a thicker rib may be available, this can be used singly, but check against the stretch guide (see General Techniques) in case the basic pattern needs to be changed before it is enlarged.

Where a double layer of fabric is used the strings of the inner head, particularly the eye-string, must be clearly indented so the shape of the head is not lost when the head cover is put on.

First size baby clothes will fit a 24″ (60cm) doll and it is a beautiful gift for older children who want to have their very own baby to play with.

Doll with jointed arms only

By combining the patterns for the jointed and traditional dolls it is possible to make a doll with jointed arms and attached legs. This variation is quick to make.

1. Make the head for the size of doll you want and then copy the appropriate pattern for the body and legs of the traditional doll and also the arm pattern belonging to the same size jointed doll. The body pattern needs to be altered at the shoulders as shown in the illustration. Draw the new line for the shoulders and neck on your pattern.

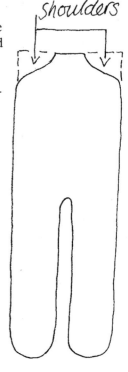

shoulders

2. Cut out the body and arms, on two thicknesses of fabric. Sew and stuff the arms following the instructions for the jointed doll. Sew all round the body and legs, leaving only the opening at the neck.

3. Stuff the body and insert the finished head into the neck opening. You may need to unpick the shoulder seams a short way to enable the head to fit inside. Sew neatly around the neck.

4. Stab stitch at crotch and feet as for the traditional doll.

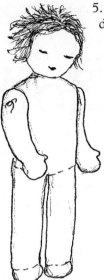

5. Attach the arms at the shoulders as described for the jointed doll.

Chapter 6

Clothes

Once the doll is finished you need to clothe it, for part of the joy of owning and playing is in dressing the doll. Clothes both identify and characterise the doll.

A doll wearing a richly coloured cloak becomes a prince, a shawl wrapped around makes a baby and a pretty dress is the signal for a party. The ritual of putting a doll into night clothes and then tucking it snugly into bed often helps a child who has difficulty in moving from active day to calm bedtime. Clothes can provide a bridge between the child's inner need for a cuddly companion and the outside world's preconceptions, for somehow it is more acceptable to play with a pirate or prince than an 'ordinary' doll. Reluctant doll owners can often be won over if the doll wears outfits recycled from their own outgrown and familiar garments.

A selection of doll's clothing and accessories are described in this chapter. The clothes are designed to fit the limbed dolls made from the patterns in this book, and are labelled as small, medium and large. Please note however that your doll will be original to you and may not be exactly the same shape or size as mine. The patterns are cut generously to allow for possible variations but always check to ensure the clothes will fit your doll. It is very disheartening to make clothes, and then discover they are too tight and have to be forced over the head and tugged to fit the body.

Doll's clothes need not take much energy or time providing a few simple guidelines are fol-

lowed. The shape of the clothes should be kept simple with the minimum of seams, and need to be easy to take on and off, the colour must be attractive and the fabric appropriate in texture and scale. It is better to produce garments from patterns based on rectangles, made in beautiful fabrics and decorated with lace, ribbon or embroidery, than to rely on complicated shapes for maximum effect. With a little help, most of the garments can be made by children themselves.

Please read the notes below on materials and techniques. To avoid unnecessary repetition various terms and instructions are explained here, rather than in the individual patterns.

Patterns

No seam allowances are included on the pattern pieces. The patterns are drawn actual size and do not need to be enlarged. Each pattern has all three sizes marked on it. Identify the pattern pieces for the garment you wish to make and trace off in the correct size for your doll. Put the pattern shapes on the fabric, placing on the fold as indicated. Draw or mark the shape accurately and cut out $^1/_2$ " (1cm) away from this line. The line you have drawn is the sewing or seam line.

Quantities

Exact quantities are not stated; a rough guide is to allow $^1/_2$yd (50cm) for clothes for the large doll and $^1/_4$yd (25cm) for the medium or small doll. Most items can be made from remnants, scraps or recycled clothing.

Fabric

Suggestions for fabrics are given with each pattern. When choosing materials consider not only aesthetic qualities such as colour, pattern and texture but also practical points. The fabric must be washable and preferably need little or no ironing. Fabric which is very thick or textured is more difficult to work and should be avoided unless you are an experienced sewer. Closely woven materials and knit fabrics are ideal, they are simple to cut out and sew and do not fray easily. Shiny, silky or pile fabrics require more care; beautiful clothes can be made from these fancy materials but they do mean more work.

I prefer to use natural materials for dolls' clothes as I feel this complements the nature of the dolls themselves, but this is not always possible, and certainly the ease of use of acrylic felt and polar fleece does make them very attractive. Some suitable fabrics are discussed below in more detail.

Felt

Acrylic felt is widely available, comes in many bright colours, does not fray at all and is wonderful for sewing projects with young children. The main drawbacks are that it does not wash, although a washable felt should soon be on

sale, and it can be very bulky for small items. Use it for accessories, such as bags and waist-coats and keep seams to a minimum.

Pure wool felt is expensive and often has to be ordered from specialist outlets.

Polar fleece

This fabric has all the advantages of felt and is also washable. It is made from recycled plastic fibres and comes in many colours. It is quite thick and best used for coats and jackets.

Knitted fabrics

Virtually all types of knitted fabrics are good for making dolls' clothes. Thin cotton knits can be used for underwear and T-shirts, more substantial knits for dresses, tops and sweatshirts, tracksuit material for trousers, skirts and jackets. Velour can also be used to make cuddly tops and trousers and is especially good for pyjamas.

When cutting out the pattern pieces make sure that the most stretch of the fabric always goes across the garment, e.g. round the waist rather than from head to toe. Most knit fabrics do not fray and need very little finishing off. Unfinished edges that are cut across the material, such as at the neck, are likely to stretch out of shape and need to be turned and sewn down.

Woven fabrics

Closely woven cottons, wools and cotton/wool mixes are ideal for making most of the garments described in this chapter. They are easy to work with and available in many different colours, patterns and textures. Some woven fabrics have a much looser weave, these are more difficult to work with and usually need to be neatened, by oversewing or zigzagging, as soon as each piece is cut out.

Synthetic fibres

In general these materials are harder to work with and not so pleasing to touch. There is a new generation of synthetics which mimic the characteristics of natural fibres and are much easier to work with. However there are times when nothing else will match the slippery satin glitter of synthetic fabrics, so use them in small amounts for princes, princesses, ballerinas and the like. Dress net is particularly useful as it provides bulk for glamorous skirts and does not fray. Be aware that synthetic fabrics are often highly flammable and must be used with care.

Pattern symbols

Straight Grain: Place the pattern parallel to the finished edge (selvedge) of the fabric.

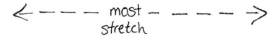

Most Stretch (knit fabrics only): Place the pattern with the most stretch of the fabric (across the rib) as indicated by the arrow.

Fold: Place the pattern on the fold of the fabric.

Centre Front: Marks the centre of the front of the pattern piece.

CF

Centre Back: Marks the centre of the back of the pattern piece.

CB

Sewing Line: The actual line on which the seam is made.

sewing line

KEY

———————— Large
——— — ——— Medium
— — — — — Small

Construction techniques

The methods outlined here are the ones most useful in terms of speed and sturdiness. They are not necessarily conventional dressmaking techniques but produce serviceable garments without too much work. Refer also to the chapter **General Techniques** which gives details of sewing stitches and other basic information.

Seams

Unless stated otherwise, **all seams should be sewn with the right sides together**. Line up the two pieces of fabric which are to be joined, and keep in place with pins or a tacking (basting) thread while you work. If you place pins at right angles to the seam (across, not parallel to the cut edges) it is possible to machine while they are still in place.

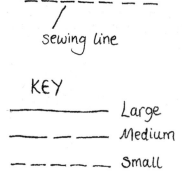
pins at right angle to edge

By hand

Use a small backstitch and be extra careful to start and finish your work with several small stitches. Never use a knot because this makes a weak place, which will eventually pull through the fabric.

backstitch

By machine

Select a small stitch and start and finish seams by reversing for $1/2''$ (1cm). Trim any loose threads as you go.

Neatening seams

Some fabrics do not fray and the raw edges can be left untreated. This is true of most knit fabrics, felt and polar fleece. Any fabric that frays must be neatened. If the material you are using has lots of loose threads at the edges it may be easier to oversew or zigzag all round each piece immediately after cutting out.

By hand

Trim the seams to ¼″ (0.5cm) and oversew together.

By machine

Trim the seams and zigzag the raw edges together.

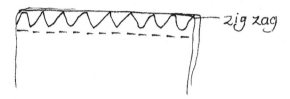

Commercial liquid

It is possible to buy a commercial preparation which is painted on and binds the fibres of the fabric together. It also stiffens the fabric and is only suitable for small areas.

Neatening garment edges

(necks, armholes etc.)

All edges of woven and knit materials need to be finished in some way and even non-fray fabrics, like felt, will be strengthened by turning and sewing.

Start by cutting off any loose threads and trim the edge so it is even with no bumps or dips.

Pinking shears

The simplest method is to use pinking shears. These are commercially manufactured scissors, which leave the cut edges shaped into small zigzags. This finish inhibits fraying but does not prevent it entirely. I would only use pinking shears on closely woven fabrics and if sewing with a young child. The results will not be as durable as if the edge is turned under and sewn down.

By hand

1. Turn the fabric to the wrong side once and then a second time, so that the raw edges are completely hidden. Fold over about ¼″ (0.5cm) each time. Pin as you go to hold the edge in place.

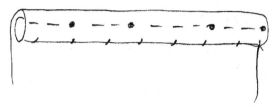

2. Sew, with a matching thread, and use a catch or hemming stitch.

By machine

1. Zigzag all round the edge.

2. Fold over ¼″ (0.5cm) of the fabric to the wrong side.

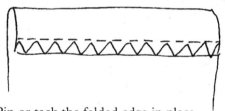

3. Pin or tack the folded edge in place and sew.
or

1. Turn the fabric to the wrong side once and then a second time, so that the raw edges are completely hidden. Fold over about ¼″ (0.5cm) each time. Pin as you go to hold the edge in place. Tack (baste) the turnings if you wish.

2. Sew through all thicknesses of fabric. You can use a straight machine stitch but I find that using a zigzag stitch for this process gives a neater finish.

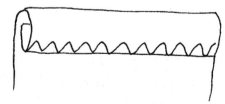

Hems

Before starting to sew the hem, cut off any loose threads and trim the hem so that it is even and 1″ (2.5cm) longer than the required length.

By hand

1. Turn the fabric to the wrong side once and then a second time, so that the raw edges are completely hidden. Fold over about ¼″ (0.5cm) the first time and ¾″ (1.5cm) the second time. Pin as you go to hold the edge in place. Tack (baste) the turnings if you wish.

2. Sew, with a matching thread, and use a catch or hemming stitch.

By machine

1. Turn the fabric to the wrong side once and then a second time, so that the raw edges are completely hidden. Fold over about ¼″ (0.5cm) the first time and ¾″ (1.5cm) the second time. Pin as you go to hold the edge in place. Tack (baste) the turnings if you wish.

2. Sew the turned over edge, using a straight stitch or a zigzag,

or

1. Zigzag the unfinished edge.

2. Fold over 1″ (2.5cm) of the fabric to the wrong side.

3. Pin or tack the folded edge in place and machine in place.

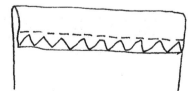

Gathering
By hand

1. Start by fastening thread securely with several small stitches.

2. Make a row of running stitches on the fabric at the seam line.

3. Pull up the thread to the required measurement. Sew a stitch to secure gathering thread.

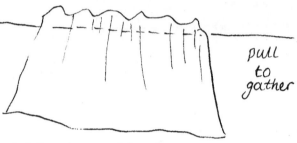

4. Adjust the material so that the gathers are evenly spaced.

By machine

1. Loosen top tension on the sewing machine and set to a long stitch length.

2. Sew on the seam line leaving long threads at beginning and end.

3. Pull bobbin thread at each end to gather the fabric to the required measurement. Tie the threads to keep gathers in place.

4. Adjust the material so that the gathers are evenly spaced.

Elastic

Two methods are described here. Unless stated otherwise in the pattern instructions, either method can be used.

To work out the length of elastic required, put the unstretched elastic round the appropriate part of the doll so it fits snugly, and cut at this point.

Direct application

Very easy and quick, best for clothes made from fine fabrics, e.g. underwear or wrist of sleeves.

1. Mark a line with pencil or tailors' chalk to show position of elastic. Measure required length of elastic and put a pin in it to mark final length. Do not cut yet.

2. Set machine to a wide zigzag and fairly long stitch.

3. Hold elastic in place at the beginning of the marked line and take several stitches to secure.

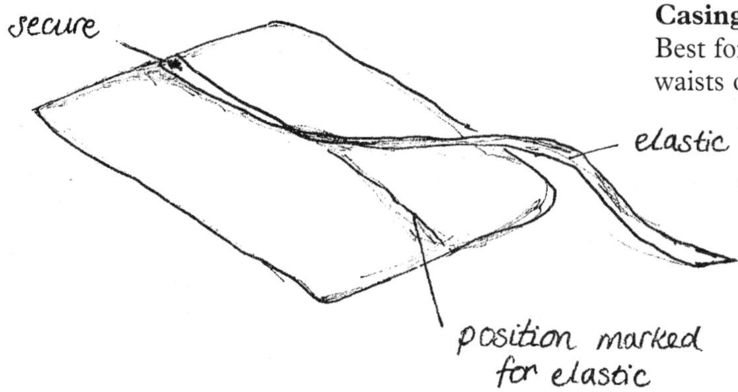

secure

elastic

position marked for elastic

4. Keep fabric smooth and pull elastic to fit. Machine the stretched elastic to the fabric, following the line you have marked. Finish with a few extra stitches to hold. Cut off excess elastic.

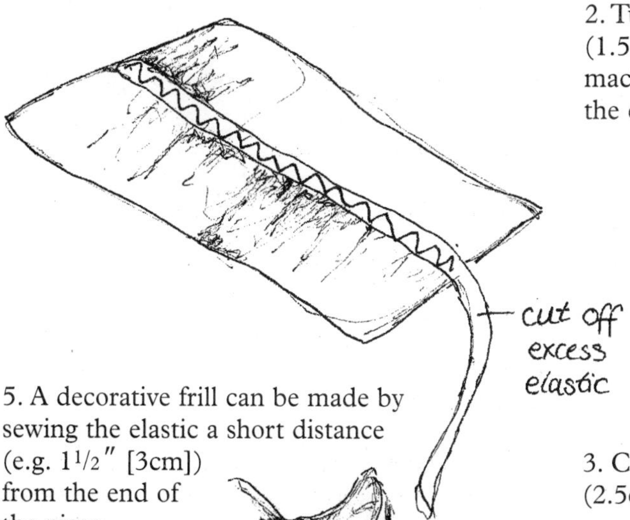

cut off excess elastic

5. A decorative frill can be made by sewing the elastic a short distance (e.g. $1^{1}/_{2}''$ [3cm]) from the end of the piece – especially useful at sleeve edges.

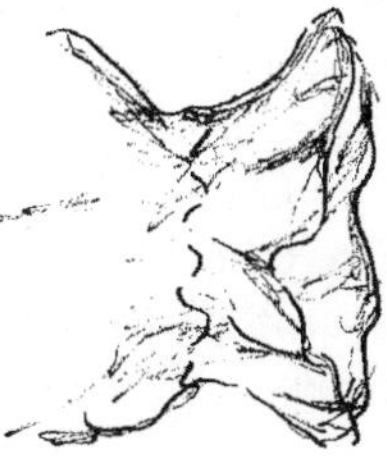

If the material is folded over and the elastic sewn to the raw edge of the folded fabric then no other sewing is needed to finish the edge.

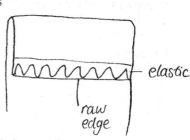

elastic

raw edge

Casing
Best for thicker fabrics and for waists of skirts and trousers.

1. Trim seams, so elastic can be threaded easily through the casing.

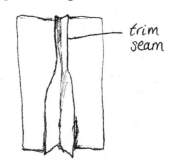

trim seam

2. Turn fabric $^{1}/_{4}''$ (0.5cm) and again $^{3}/_{4}''$ (1.5cm). Pin or tack in place and sew by machine or hand leaving a $1''$ (2.5cm) gap so the elastic can be inserted.

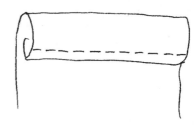

3. Cut elastic to length required plus $1''$ (2.5cm).

4. Fasten a safety pin (nappy or diaper pins are ideal) to one end of the elastic and thread though the casing.

5. Overlap the ends of the elastic and sew together securely.

6. Sew across the gap in the casing.

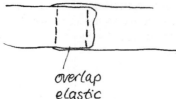

overlap
elastic

Fastenings

Various methods of fastening can be used to finish the clothing. It is important that the closure chosen is strong and also easy for a child to use. I find 'Velcro' or other similar commercial closures are quick to apply and simple to use, even by small children. For older children, button and loop fastenings, ribbon ties or press-studs (snap fasteners) are also very practical.

Velcro

'Velcro' or 'Touch 'n Close' fastenings are sold by the inch or centimetre. They consist of two flat narrow strips which interlock together but can also be peeled apart and separated. This is ideal for dolls' clothing because it is a quick-to-sew fastener that can be easily manipulated by little fingers. The strips of fastener do not fray and can be cut to the size required. If it is difficult to buy narrow strips then wider strips can be cut down their length as necessary.

Application

1. Cut small strips of Velcro – maximum size about $1/2''$ x $1''$ (1cm x 2.5cm) – and sew by hand or machine onto the opening. One piece is sewn to the right side and one to the wrong side of the opening.

2. Attach the strip either by sewing all round with a straight machine stitch or a backstitch, or sew one row of zigzag stitches down the centre.

3. Buttons, bows or other decorative features can be sewn on to the garment after the Velcro fastening is stitched in place.

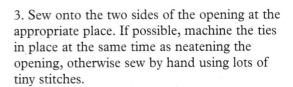

Ribbon ties

1. Cut two pieces of narrow ribbon for each tie. Each piece should be at least $8''$ (20cm).

2. If the ribbon frays, then the raw edge should be neatened. Oversew by hand or paint on a commercial liquid.

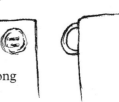

3. Sew onto the two sides of the opening at the appropriate place. If possible, machine the ties in place at the same time as neatening the opening, otherwise sew by hand using lots of tiny stitches.

Buttons

All buttons need to be sewn in place very securely and checked frequently to make sure they are not coming loose.

Loops

1 Sew the button in place.

2. On the opposite side of the opening make a thread loop using two strands of a strong thread.

3. For extra strength, sew all round the loop, using a buttonhole stitch and strong thread.

Buttonholes

1. Mark the position of the buttonhole and cut a slit slightly larger than the button. Check that the button will go through the opening easily.

2. Thread a needle with strong thread, either buttonhole stitch or two strands of sewing cotton.

3. Using a buttonhole stitch, sew all round the slit.

4. Make a bar at the bottom by sewing a row of buttonhole stitches across the end of the buttonhole.

Buttonholes can also be sewn by machine, follow the instructions given by the manufacturer of your sewing machine.

Commercial fastenings

Press studs, snaps, hooks and eyes, snap-on fasteners and press stud tape can all be used as closures for dolls' clothing. Apply to the garment following the instructions on the packet. Do check that the eventual owner of the doll's clothing can manipulate the fastener and also that any small pieces are sewn on very securely.

Decorative features

A small amount of decoration can make all the difference to a simple garment. Choose the colours and size of the trimmings with care and you will have a beautiful piece of clothing. It is usually easier to add trimmings or embroidery to a flat piece of fabric and then make up as required.

Machine embroidery

This is a good occasion to use all those fancy stitches on your sewing machine. Use a thread in a contrasting colour and follow the instructions from your own machine. Practise on a scrap of fabric before sewing on the clothes.

Hand embroidery

Simple stitches in bright colours look very effective; for example two or three rows of running stitch around the borders of a waistcoat (vest) or skirt. Consult a reference book for other embroidery stitches.

Ribbon

Pin ribbon in place and sew down on each side. This looks best interspersed with rows of tucks or sewn above a row of lace.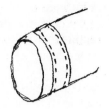

Tucks

Sew the tucks before making up the garment. Allow extra fabric for the tuck. Each tuck uses about $1/2''$ (1cm) of fabric. Tucks are most effective in groups of two or three, either on the front of a top or parallel to the lower edge of a skirt.

1. Fold the fabric over at the place you want the tuck to be. Press the folded edge to keep in place.

2. Sew through the folded fabric about $1/4''$ (0.5cm) from the edge.

By machine: Use the side of the foot on your machine as a guide and keep the line of stitches as straight as possible.

By hand: Sew with small running stitches.

3. Repeat for each tuck

4. Press flat

Lace

Pre-gathered lace or flat lace can be bought in many different widths and colours.

1. Pre-gathered lace can be sewn on the centre of a dress or top, or in single or multiple rows at intervals on a skirt.

2. Pin in place and sew in place.

Flat lace

1. Neaten the edge where the lace is to be applied with a zigzag stitch or by making a small hem.

2. Position the lace on the wrong side of the fabric so the straight edge of the lace overlaps the finished edge by ¹/₄″ (0.5cm).

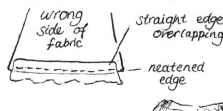

3. Sew in place

Clothes

Circle dress

The easiest possible dress: it can be made without any sewing and to fit any size doll. A perfect first item for a child to make. My own daughters were delighted to discover this 'instant' dress and spent many hours making variations for their dolls. Long dresses were nightgowns or party dresses, shorter versions worn as sun dresses or pinafores (jumpers). They embroidered brightly coloured flowers, painted pictures on the front (using watercolours; it comes out in the wash, but they didn't mind) or sewed on lace, ribbons and braids. They adapted the pattern by cutting new shapes at the neck, sleeves and hem and the dolls wore several layers of these dresses to create many different outfits.

Fabric suggestions

Woven cotton in a fine or medium weight. Plain or self-coloured material or with an overall pattern. Fabric with stripes or a one way design is not suitable.

Instructions

1. Measure the doll from the neck to the desired length of the dress. Add 2″ (5cm) to this amount. You need to cut a square of fabric with each side measuring twice this length (dress length + 2″ [5cm] x 2).

2. Fold your fabric in half and then in half again.

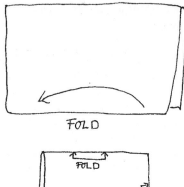

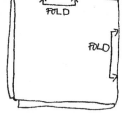

3. Mark and cut out a quarter circle, using the measurement from #1 as the radius.

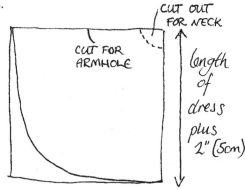

4. Cut a small piece out at the centre for the neck.

5. Cut as shown to make an armhole.

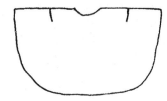

6. Neaten all raw edges, either using pinking shears or sewing by hand or machine.

7. Place on the doll; adjust fabric and tie around the waist with a ribbon or strip of fabric.

Tabard

A loose tabard can be made in a similar way from a rectangle of material. See the clothes section of the **Soft Dolls** chapter for further instructions.

Petticoat/Dress/Pinafore

This two-piece pattern is very versatile. It can be made from an attractive cotton print and worn as a summer dress, or sewn in a thicker cloth and worn over a long sleeved top or frock as a pinafore or jumper. Finally a sweet little petticoat can be made from plain cotton lawn with some lace trimmings applied.

Fabric suggestions
Petticoat: Fine woven cotton, best in a pale colour. Ribbon and lace for decoration.

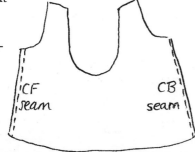

Dress: Fine or medium weight woven cotton. Bold or flowery patterns are equally effective.

Pinafore:
Medium weight woven cotton or thin wool fabric. Plain material, small checks or tweeds look good.

Instructions
1. Cut out 2 fronts and 2 backs, from the pattern on the next page.

2. Sew the centre front and centre back seams.

3. Neaten the neck edges.

4. Neaten the armhole edges.

5. Sew the shoulder seams.

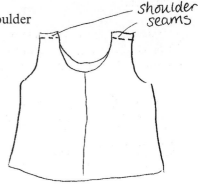

shoulder seams

6. Hem the lower edge.

Variations
Petticoat: Add rows of lace and ribbon to lower edge or sew a wide, gathered strip of lace to the centre front seam.

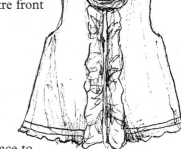

Dress: Apply lace to the bottom edge and/or to the neck and armhole edges.

Pinafore: Embroider, by hand or machine, a simple design either side of the front seam.

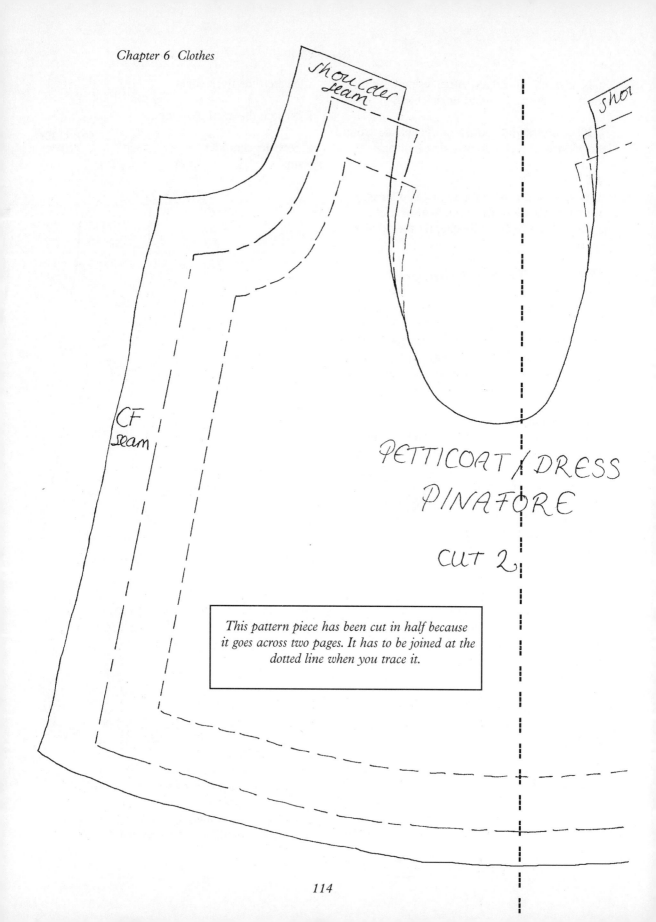

shoulder seam

sho...

CF seam

PETTICOAT/DRESS
PINAFORE

CUT 2

This pattern piece has been cut in half because it goes across two pages. It has to be joined at the dotted line when you trace it.

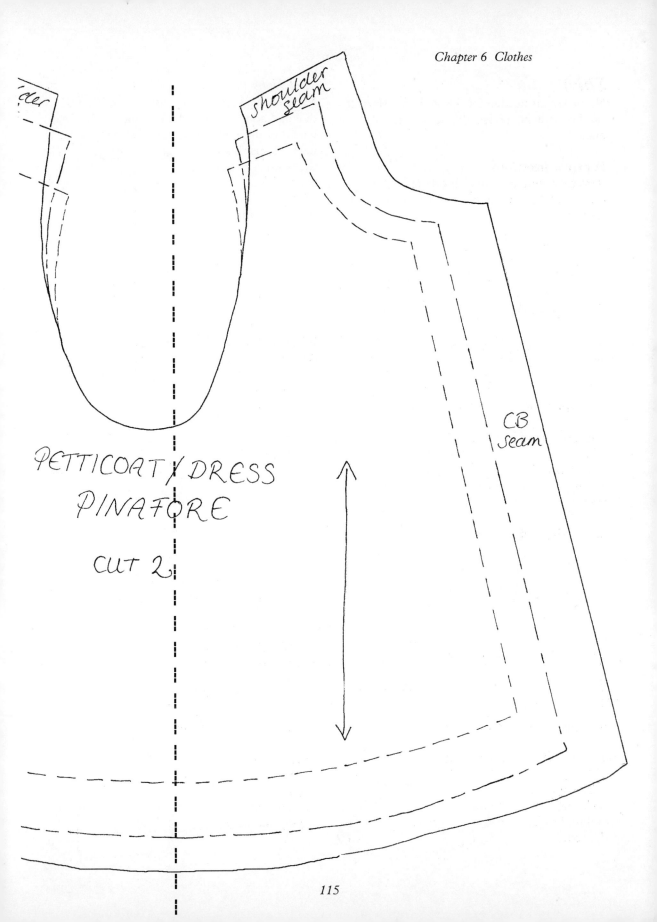

der

shoulder
seam

CB
seam

PETTICOAT/DRESS
PINAFORE

CUT 2

Skirt

No pattern is needed for this gathered skirt. It can be made in any length and is quick to make.

Fabric suggestions

Woven or knitted cottons, broderie anglaise or other lacy cloth, corduroy, needlecord in patterns or plains.

Instructions

1. Decide on the finished length of the skirt and add 2½″ (6cm) for turnings. Cut a rectangle of fabric with this measurement as the short side and the long side as indicated below:

large	30″ (75cm)
medium	25″ (60cm)
small	20″ (50cm)

Example: for a skirt for a medium sized doll

Finished length is to be 4½″ (11cm)
add   2½″ (6cm)
Final length is   7″ (17.5cm)
You need to cut a rectangle 7″ x 25″ (11cm x 60cm)

2. Sew short edges together.

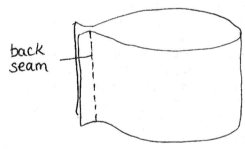

back seam

3. Make a casing at the waist and insert elastic or apply elastic directly to top edge.

4. Sew a hem at the lower edge.

5. Decorate with tucks, lace or embroidery as desired.

Variations

Panties: Measure from waist to crotch on the doll and add 3½″ (17.5cm), which is the final length of the skirt. Make skirt following the instructions. Taking the seam as centre back, fold the skirt in half to find the centre front. Match these two points and sew front and back together on the right side for ½″ (1cm) each side of the centre point.

sew

centre front/ centre back

Ruffled skirt: Decide on the depth of the finished ruffle or frill (e.g. 2″ [5cm]) and subtract from final length of skirt. Make skirt following the instructions but do not finish the lower edge. Cut ruffle twice the width of the skirt, joining fabric as necessary. Finish the bottom edge with a hem and lace. Gather the top edge, pull up gathers to fit the lower edge of the skirt and sew to skirt.

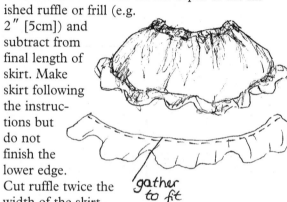

gather to fit skirt

Top/Dress/Jacket

A versatile pattern that can be used to make blouses, shirts, dresses and jackets. It is cut in one piece from folded cloth and so has a minimum of seams. A doll wearing a dress or top with a simple gathered pinafore (as made for the soft doll) looks very special and the whole outfit can be made very quickly and easily.

Fabric suggestions

Medium weight woven cotton, self-coloured or with a small pattern, not suitable for one way designs.

Instructions

1. Fold fabric in half and then in half again. Cut out pattern on the following pages so both edges are on a fold. Cut open at centre back.

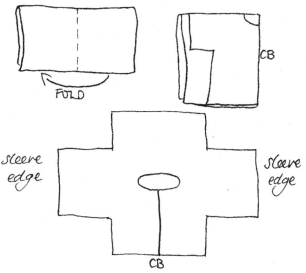

FOLD

CB

sleeve edge

sleeve edge

CB

2. Neaten the raw edges at the back and apply fastening.

3. Neaten neck opening.

4. Make a hem at sleeve edge.

5. Sew underarm seam from waist to wrist.

wrist

sewing line

waist

6. Make a hem at the lower edge.

Variations

Blouse or shirt: Cut open at centre front not centre back. Add collar using pattern and instructions as for coat. Follow instructions as for top; sew small buttons over front fastenings.

Dress: Lengthen pattern as desired. Cut down only 3 - 4″ (7.5 - 10cm) at centre back. At #3 also directly apply elastic at neck but otherwise follow the instructions as for the top.

Simple dress:
Lengthen pattern as desired. Do not cut an opening at the back but enlarge the opening at the neck until it is big enough for the doll's head to fit through.

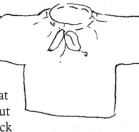

Complete as for the top, omitting all instructions referring to the back or neck opening. Finish the raw edge at the neck by turning 1/4″ (0.5cm) to the inside and, using embroidery thread, sew a line of running stitches all round the neck. Leave long threads at the start and finish and tie a knot at each end of the thread. Put dress on doll; draw up neck to fit doll and tie threads in a bow.

Sleeves:
a) Separate sleeve - cut pattern straight up at beginning of arm and cut out as separate pieces, remember to add seam allowances. Sew sleeve to main top and then proceed as for top. Useful if you only have a small piece of fabric or where using striped material.

cut here for separate sleeve

b) Frilly cuff - lengthen sleeve by 2 - 3″ (5 - 7.5cm). Fold this extra material in half and directly apply elastic. Complete as for top.

elastic

sleeve

fold for frilly cuff

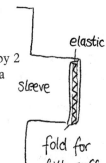

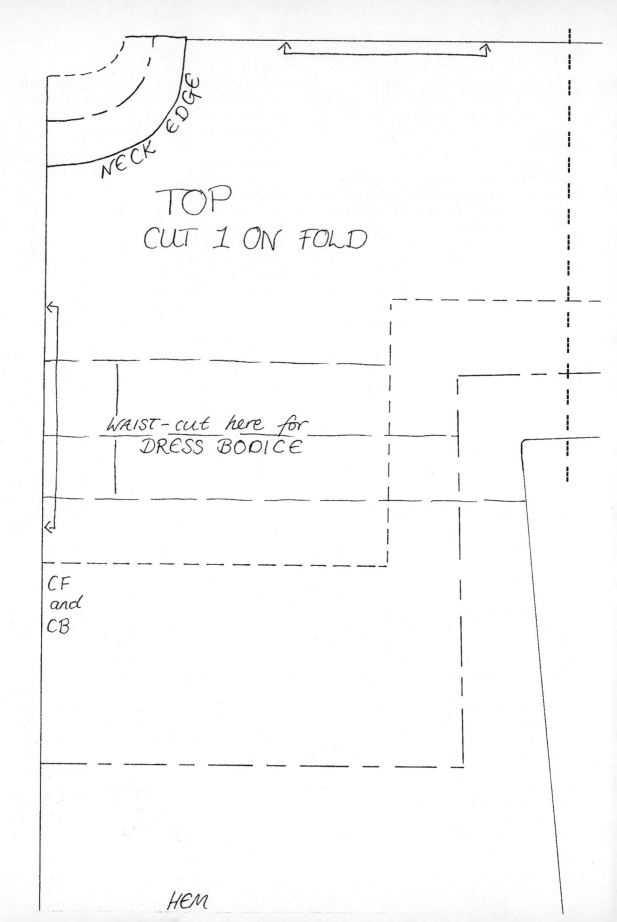

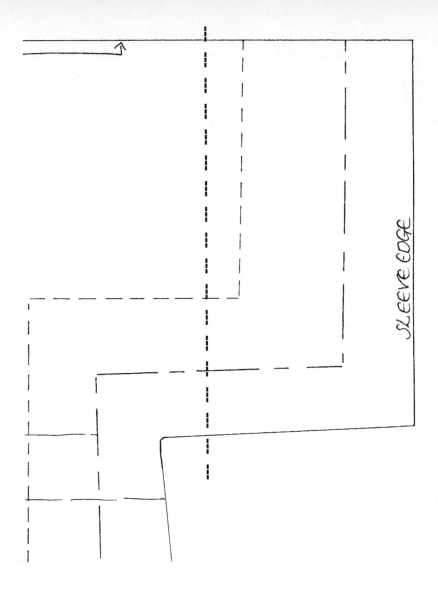

SLEEVE EDGE

This pattern piece has been cut in half because
it goes across two pages. It has to be joined at the
dotted line when you trace it.

Jacket: Cut open at centre front not centre back. Shape fronts into a V-neck if wished.

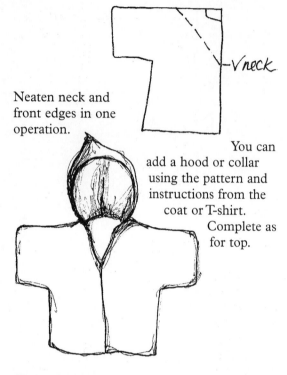

—Vneck

Neaten neck and front edges in one operation.

You can add a hood or collar using the pattern and instructions from the coat or T-shirt.
Complete as for top.

Dress with gathered skirt/ Party dress

A pretty dress that uses the pattern for the top as its base. It can be made into a beautiful party dress by adding lots of ribbon and lace.

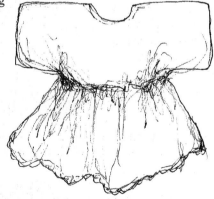

Fabric suggestions
Medium or fine woven cotton. Silk dupion, satins or taffeta for the party dress.

Instructions

1. Adapt the pattern for the top by cutting off at the waist (about 1″ [2.5cm] below start of sleeve). Lengthen the sleeves by 2 - 3″ (5 - 7.5cm) if you want to have a frill at the wrist. Cut out the bodice from the new pattern you have just made.

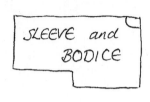

SLEEVE and BODICE

2. Neaten neck edge.

3. Neaten sleeve ends. For frill, turn 1″ (1½″) or 2.5cm (3.5cm) to wrong side at sleeve end. Apply elastic.

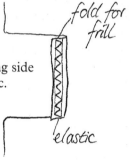

fold for frill

elastic

4. Sew underarm seam.

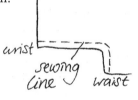

wrist *sewing line* *waist*

5. For the skirt, cut a rectangle of fabric according to the measurements below

large	40″ x 6″ (100cm x 15cm)
medium	32″ x 5½″ (80cm x 14cm)
small	28″ x 4½″ (70cm x 12cm)

Join the material if necessary to get a long enough piece.

6. Make a hem at the lower edge of the skirt. *Optional*: add lace.

7. Gather the top edge of the skirt.

gather

Pull up gathers to fit the bodice, making sure the gathers are evenly spaced. Pin and sew to the waist seam.

8. Neaten the back opening, adding fastenings at neck and waist.

Variations

Party dress: Choose a beautiful fabric. Many fine materials fray easily so, to prevent this, zigzag around each piece before beginning. Use the pattern as described above but cut the sleeves and the skirt longer and wider. Neaten the lower edges of the sleeves and skirt. Make several tucks parallel to these edges and sew on lace and rows of ribbon. A strip of gathered lace could be sewn on at the centre front and at the neck edge.

Trousers

Fabric suggestions
Medium weight woven cotton, corduroy, lightweight denim, tracksuit fabric, velour.

Instructions
1. Cut out 2 trouser pieces from the pattern on the following pages. Note which part is the leg and which the crotch.

2. Sew the crotch seams, joining the two pieces at centre front and centre back.

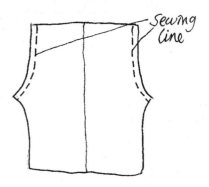

3. Elasticate the waist. A casing is best if you are using thicker fabrics.

4. Finish the bottom hems.

5. Sew the leg seam. Sew this in one continuous seam, starting at the bottom of one leg, up to crotch and back down the other leg.

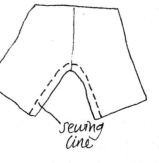

Variations
Tracksuit trousers: Make from knitted jersey fabric and sew elastic at the ankles when finishing the bottom hems. Complete as for trousers.

Shorts: Cut pattern as indicated. Use lightweight cotton fabric and follow the instructions above.

Frilly knickers: Make as for shorts but add elastic and lace to lower edges of legs.

This pattern piece has been cut in half because it goes across two pages. It has to be joined at the dotted line when you trace it.

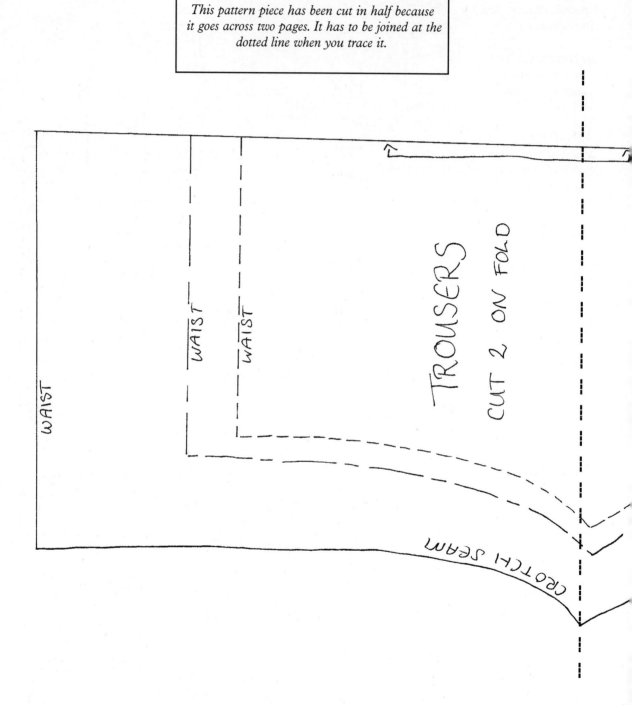

TROUSERS

CUT 2 ON FOLD

WAIST

WAIST

WAIST

WAIST

CROTCH SEAM

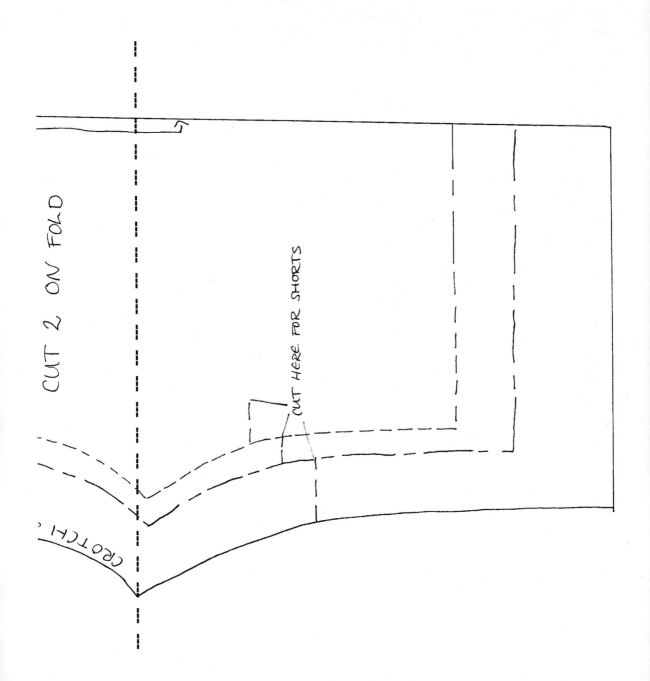

CUT 2 ON FOLD

CROTCH

CUT HERE FOR SHORTS

T-shirts

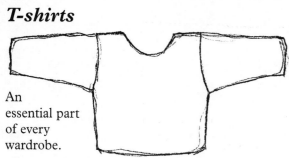

An
essential part
of every
wardrobe.

Fabric suggestions
Suitable for knitted fabrics only; cotton jersey,
velour or tracksuit material. Used clothing is a
good source of attractive material and you may
be able to recycle the knitted bands at neck and
wrists.

Instructions
1. Cut out 1 back, 1 front and 2 sleeves from
knit fabric.

2. Sew back to front at shoulders. Try on the
doll, but do not overstretch the neckline. Cut

an opening
at centre
back if the neck is not large
enough.

3. Neaten and add fastenings
to back opening if necessary.

4. Neaten neck edge.

5. Sew sleeves to armhole. Match the centre
mark on the sleeve to the shoulder seam and
ease to fit.

6. Neaten
lower edge of sleeve.

7. Sew underarm seam
from lower edge of body
to end of sleeve.

8. Finish the
lower edge.

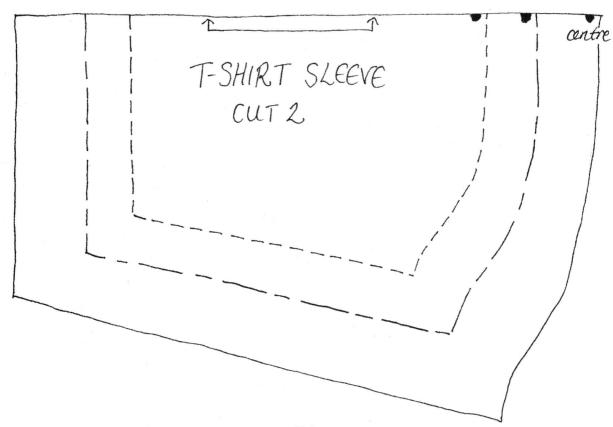

T-SHIRT SLEEVE
CUT 2

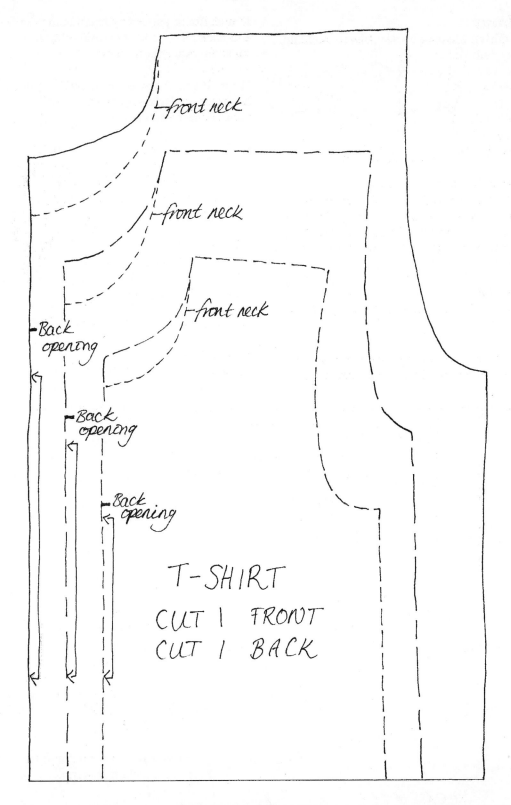

front neck

front neck

front neck

Back opening

Back opening

Back opening

T-SHIRT
CUT 1 FRONT
CUT 1 BACK

Variations

Sweatshirt: Make in tracksuit fabric and add bands of rib knit at wrists, waist and neck. Measure where band is to be applied (B) and sew in place instead of neatening edges. To do this, cut rectangles of rib with a length of about three-quarters of the measurement (B) and with a width of 2 - 3″ (5 - 8cm). Fold rib in half along its length. Sew the doubled rib to garment with a stretch or small zigzag stitch, stretching rib to fit as you go.

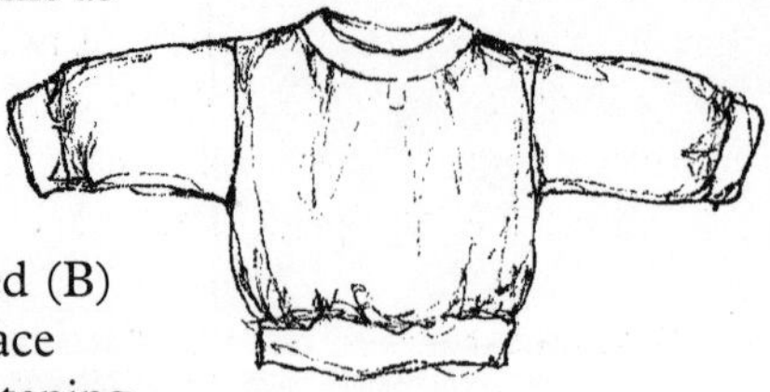

Dress: Adapt pattern by lengthening the front and back pieces and shortening the sleeves. Make up as for the T-shirt.

Hooded top: A pattern is given for a medium hood, for the large size add 2″ (5cm) to front and neck edges, for the small size take off 1″ (2.5cm) at the front and neck.

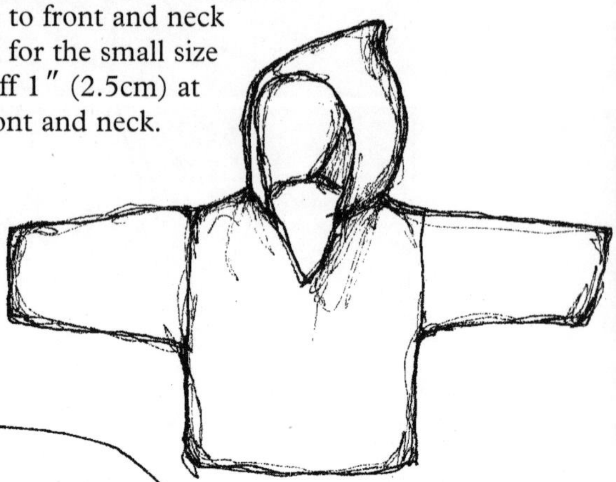

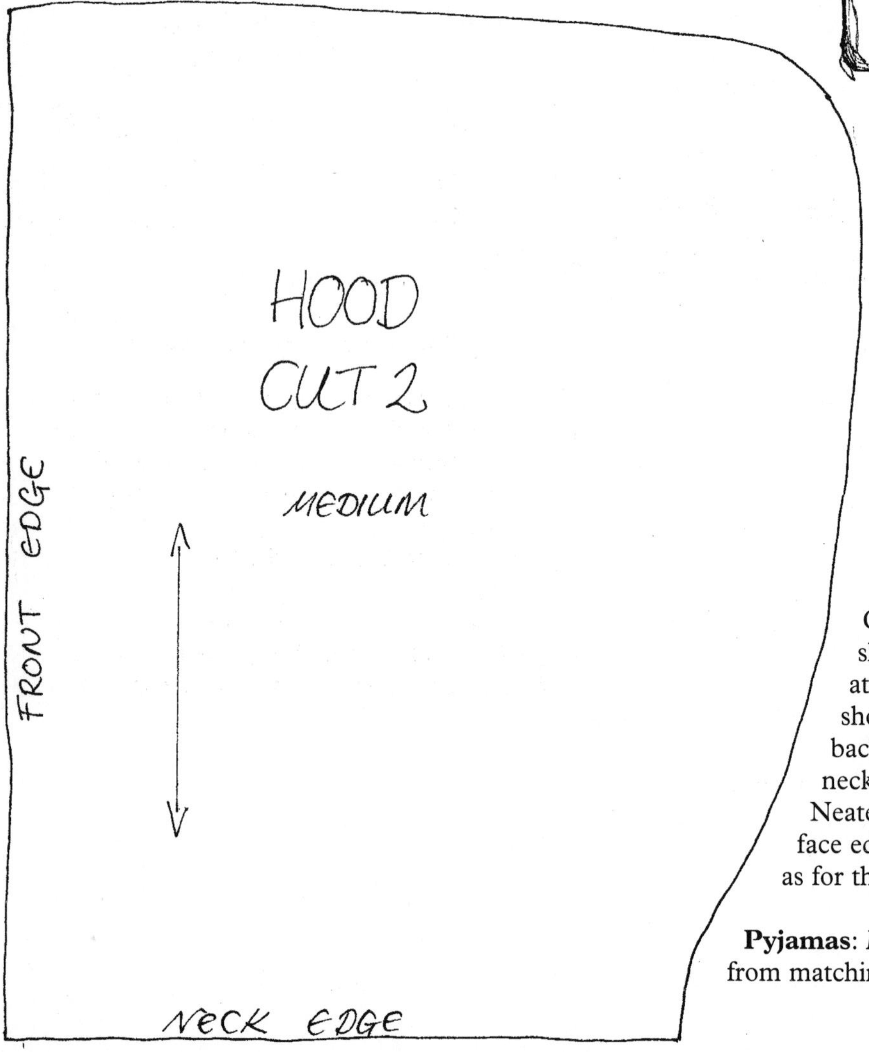

HOOD

CUT 2

MEDIUM

FRONT EDGE

NECK EDGE

Cut out top as for T-shirt and cut an opening at centre front. Sew shoulder seams of top and back seam of hood. Sew neck of hood to neck of top. Neaten front opening and face edge of hood. Continue as for the top.

Pyjamas: Make top and trousers from matching material.

Waistcoat

A little waistcoat or vest gives the finishing touch to any outfit. This is a one-piece pattern that can be made from felt in minutes.

Fabric suggestions

Felt, polar fleece, soft leather, corduroy or any medium weight woven cotton.

Instructions

1. Cut out the waistcoat, from the pattern on pages 128 - 9, placing the pattern on the fold of the fabric.

2. Sew the shoulder seams.

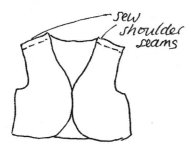

3. Neaten all raw edges.

4. *Optional*: embroider a pretty motif on the front or sew a line of embroidery round the edges.

Variations

1. **Felt**: When made from felt or other non-fray material there is no need to neaten edges. Cut out from the pattern but do not add seam allowances except at the shoulders. Sew the shoulder seams. This is extra easy and is an ideal first sewing project for a child.

2. **Side seams**: Separate pattern on dotted line and cut out 1 back on fold and 2 fronts. Sew the side seams and then follow the main instructions. Useful where fabric is limited.

3. **Lined**: Cut 1 in main fabric and 1 in lining. Put wrong sides together and sew round armholes, back neck and outside edge.

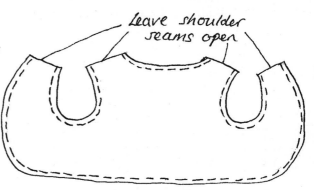

Turn to right side through one shoulder. Press the garment so that it lies flat. Sew the shoulder seams together so that you have 4 layers of material at each side. Press the waistcoat to flatten seams.
Optional: topstitch round all edges.

4. **Pockets**: Cut a square of fabric $1\frac{1}{2}''$ ($2''/2\frac{1}{2}''$) or 3cm (4cm/5cm). Neaten all 4 sides and sew onto the front of waistcoat.

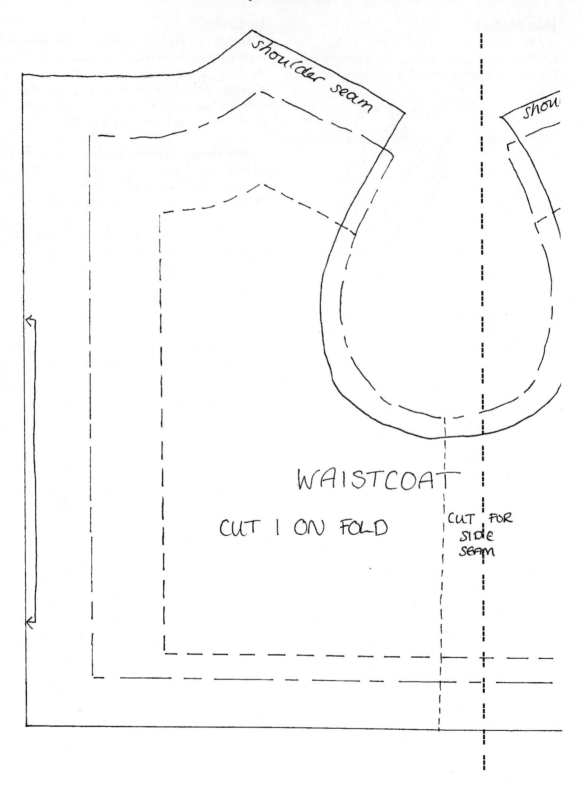

shoulder seam

shou

WAISTCOAT

CUT 1 ON FOLD

CUT FOR
SIDE
SEAM

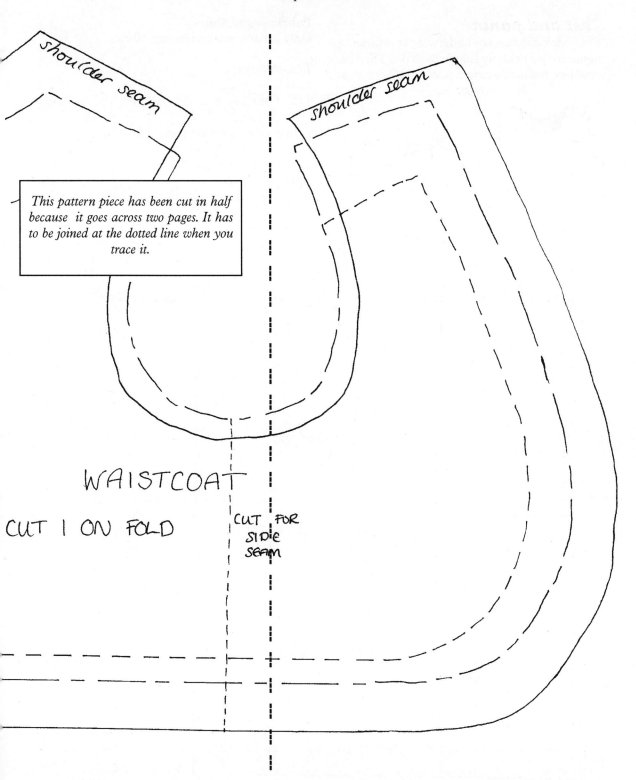

shoulder seam

shoulder seam

This pattern piece has been cut in half because it goes across two pages. It has to be joined at the dotted line when you trace it.

WAISTCOAT

CUT 1 ON FOLD

CUT FOR SIDE SEAM

Vest and pants

Every doll needs some underwear and these items are particularly simple to make. The vest could be made in a bright print and worn as a summer top.

Fabric suggestions

Only suitable for cotton knit fabrics.

Instructions
Vest

1. Cut out 1 front and 1 back, both on the fold.

2. Sew shoulder seams and side seams.

3. Neaten, with a small zigzag stitch, all the raw edges.

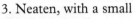

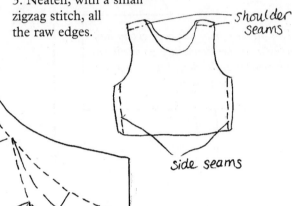

shoulder seams

side seams

cut for front

VEST
CUT 1
FRONT
AND 1 BACK
ON FOLD

<----- most stretch ----->

Pants

1. Fold material in half and then in half again. Cut out pattern so both crotch and centre front/back are on a fold.

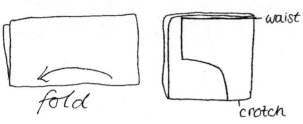

fold

waist

crotch

2. Neaten the leg openings using a small zigzag stitch.

3. Sew the side seams.

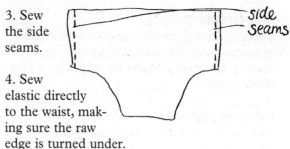

side seams

4. Sew elastic directly to the waist, making sure the raw edge is turned under.

Other suggestions for underwear:
Pants: See variations under skirts and trousers.

Petticoat: See separate pattern.

Waist slip or petticoat: Make as for skirt.

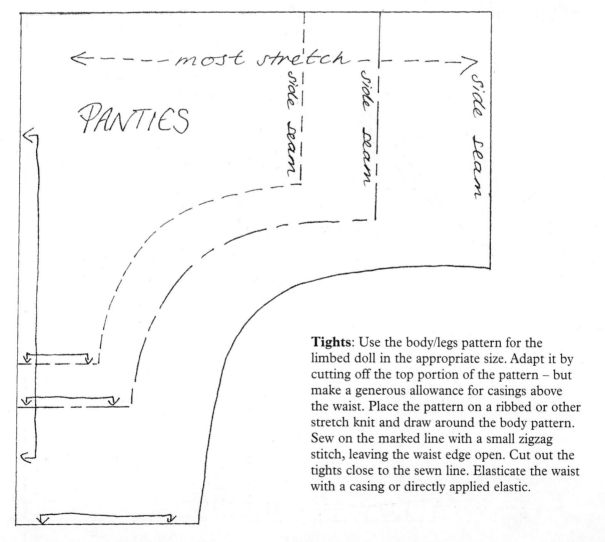

most stretch

PANTIES

side seam

side seam

side seam

Tights: Use the body/legs pattern for the limbed doll in the appropriate size. Adapt it by cutting off the top portion of the pattern – but make a generous allowance for casings above the waist. Place the pattern on a ribbed or other stretch knit and draw around the body pattern. Sew on the marked line with a small zigzag stitch, leaving the waist edge open. Cut out the tights close to the sewn line. Elasticate the waist with a casing or directly applied elastic.

Nightwear

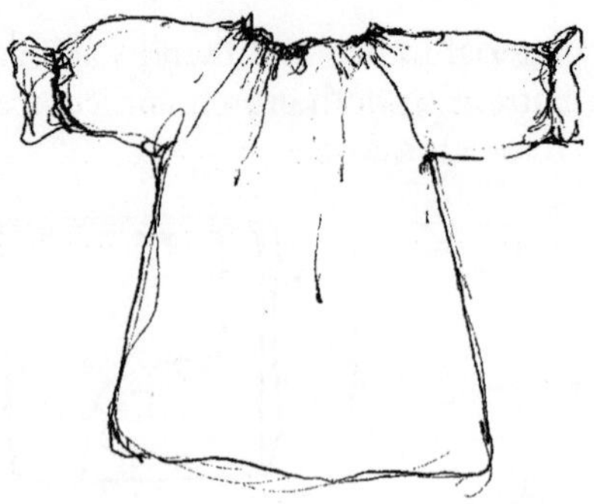

Children often like to mimic their own routine and put their doll to bed, and a pretty night-dress or attractive pyjamas are an essential part of the process.

Fabric suggestions

Soft light or medium weight cottons, or mixtures of cotton and wool fibres, brushed cotton or winceyette. Velour, stretch towelling or cotton knits for pyjamas.

Instructions
Night-dress

1. Cut out all the pattern pieces from folded material. You should have 1 front, 1 back and 2 sleeves.

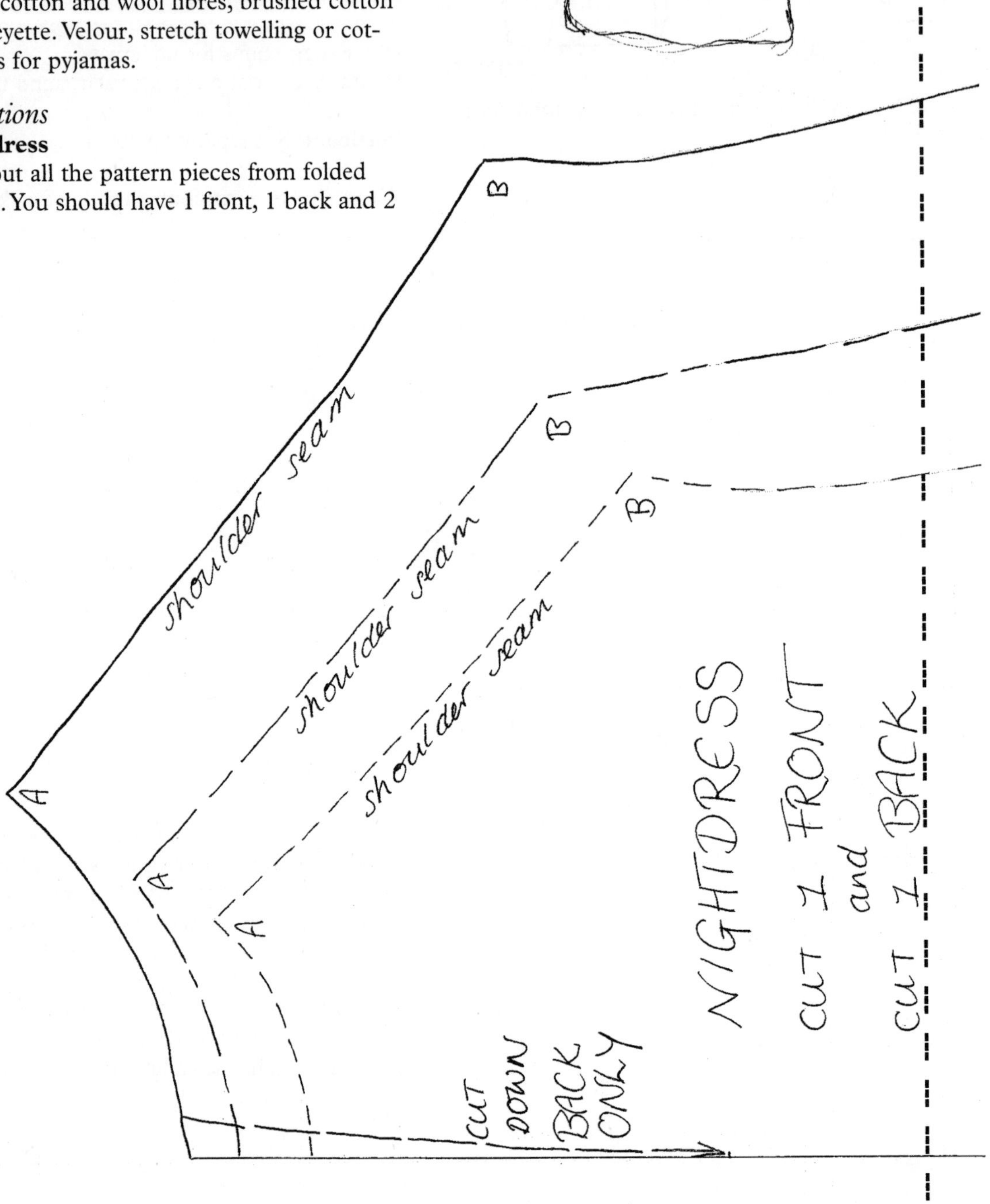

shoulder seam

shoulder seam

shoulder seam

shoulder seam

B

B

B

A

A

A

NIGHTDRESS

CUT 1 FRONT

and

CUT 1 BACK

CUT DOWN BACK ONLY

This pattern piece has been cut in half because it goes across two pages. It has to be joined at the dotted line when you trace it.

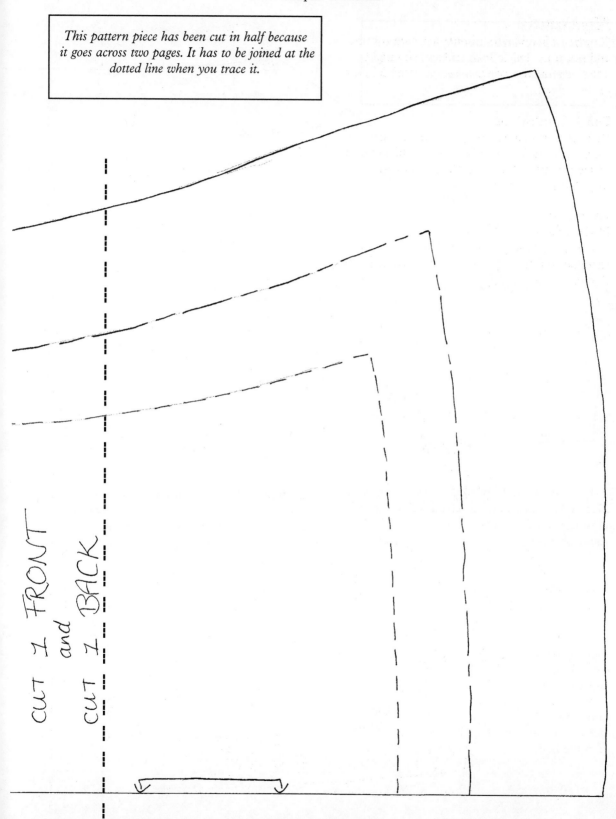

CUT 1 FRONT
and
CUT 1 BACK

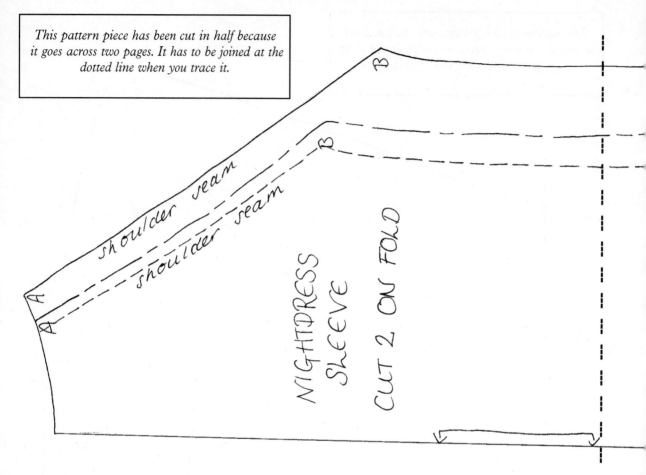

This pattern piece has been cut in half because it goes across two pages. It has to be joined at the dotted line when you trace it.

shoulder seam

shoulder seam

NIGHTDRESS SLEEVE CUT 2 ON FOLD

2. Cut as indicated for centre back opening. Neaten back opening and attach Velcro or other closing 1″ (2.5cm) down from the neck edge.

3. Sew sleeves to back and front pieces as indicated.

4. Turn under ½″ (1cm) at top edge and sew elastic all round the neck, using the direct application method.

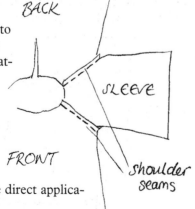

BACK

SLEEVE

FRONT

shoulder seams

5. Turn under ¾″ (1.5cm) at bottom of the sleeves and sew elastic to wrist. Use the direct application method and make sure the raw edges are sewn under the elastic.

6. Sew side seams starting at the lower end of the sleeve and finishing at the bottom of the nightdress.

7. Sew hem.

wrist

sewing line

hem

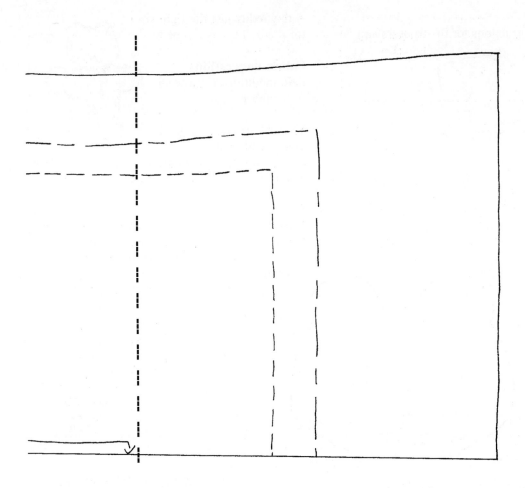

8. *Optional*: add lace at centre front, lower edge and/or round the neck and wrists.

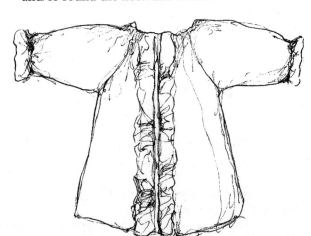

Variations

Dress: Shorten the pattern and make in a bright cotton fabric with matching knickers for an attractive summer outfit.

Pyjamas
Follow the instructions for the trousers and
T-shirt or top.

A tiny teddy just the right size
for the doll to take to bed.

Fabric suggestions
Felt, medium weight wool
or fur fabric.

You will also need a small
quantity of stuffing
(sheepswool), some embroidery thread in a dark
colour and a short length of narrow ribbon.

Instructions
1. Place pattern on a double layer of fabric. The
fabric should have the right sides inside. Draw
around the outline on the wrong side. Do not
cut out.

CUT OUT
AFTER
SEWING

**Teddy
Bear**

TEDDY | CUT 2

slit
at
back

2. Sew all the way round the
teddy shape.

3. Cut out the teddy ¼″
(0.5cm) away from the
stitching line.

4. Cut a slit at the centre back, as indicated
on the pattern.

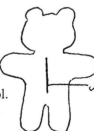

slit

5. Turn to right side
and stuff with sheepswool.

6. Sew the back opening
together with tiny stitches.

7. Embroider the features, using the illustration as a guide. Tie a ribbon round the neck.

Fabric suggestions
Corduroy, medium weight wool or polar fleece.

Coat

This coat can be made with a collar or a hood and is large enough to be worn over other clothes.

Instructions

1. Cut out all the pattern pieces. You should have 2 sleeves and 1 back, all cut from folded material, and 2 fronts plus either 2 collars or 2 hoods.

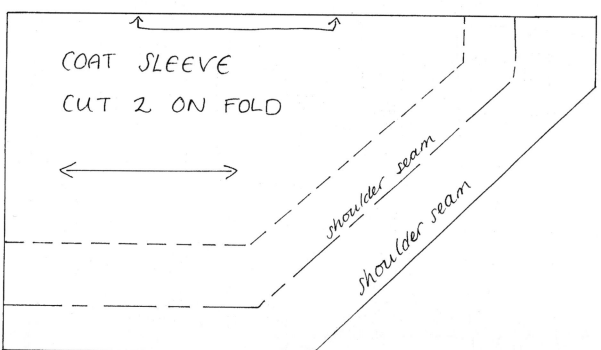

COAT SLEEVE
CUT 2 ON FOLD

shoulder seam

shoulder seam

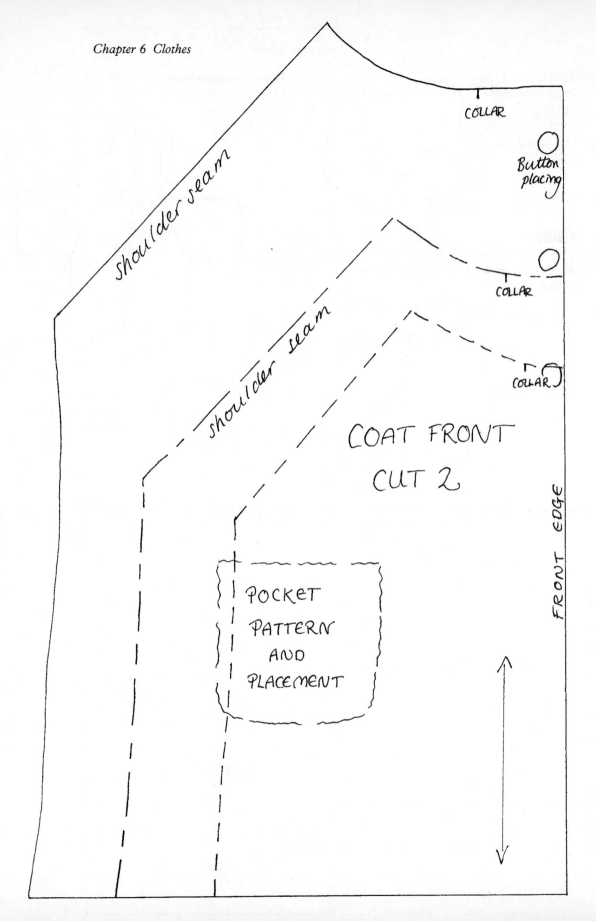

COLLAR

Button placing

COLLAR

Shoulder seam

Shoulder seam

COLLAR

COAT FRONT

CUT 2

FRONT EDGE

POCKET
PATTERN
AND
PLACEMENT

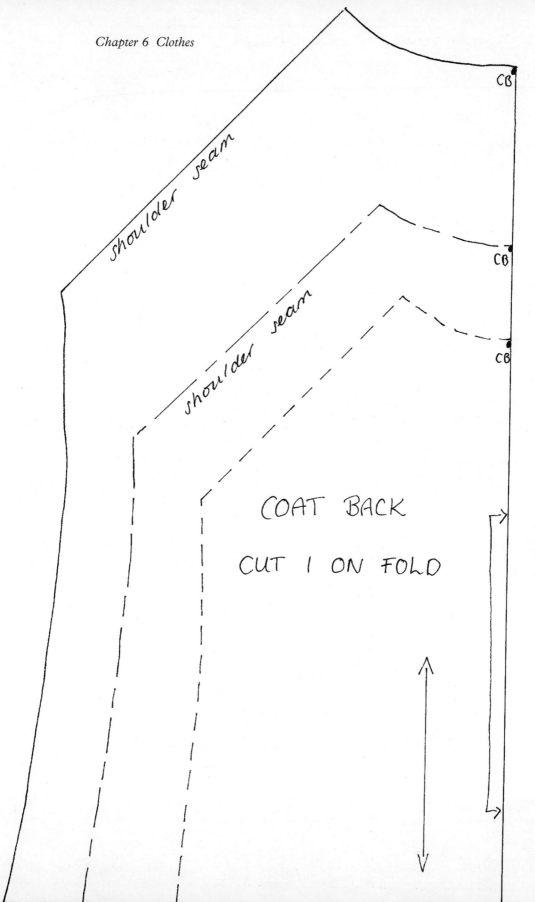

Shoulder seam

Shoulder seam

CB

CB

CB

COAT BACK

CUT 1 ON FOLD

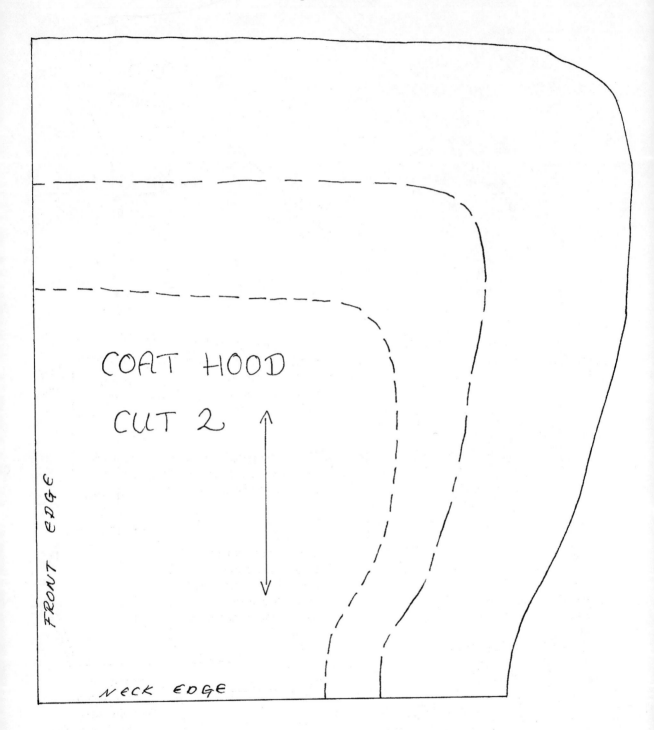

COAT HOOD

CUT 2

FRONT EDGE

NECK EDGE

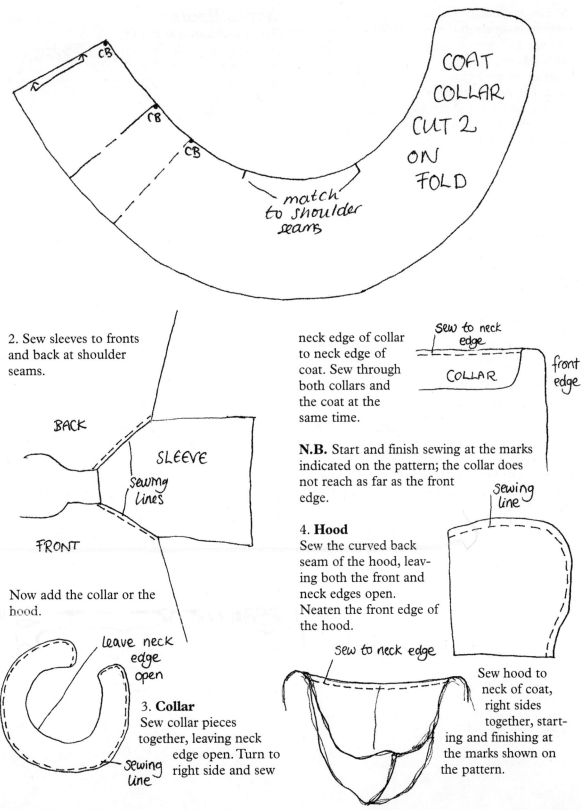

COAT COLLAR CUT 2 ON FOLD

CB
CB
CB

match to shoulder seams

2. Sew sleeves to fronts and back at shoulder seams.

BACK

SLEEVE

sewing lines

FRONT

Now add the collar or the hood.

leave neck edge open

sewing line

neck edge of collar to neck edge of coat. Sew through both collars and the coat at the same time.

N.B. Start and finish sewing at the marks indicated on the pattern; the collar does not reach as far as the front edge.

sew to neck edge

COLLAR

front edge

3. **Collar**
Sew collar pieces together, leaving neck edge open. Turn to right side and sew

4. **Hood**
Sew the curved back seam of the hood, leaving both the front and neck edges open. Neaten the front edge of the hood.

sewing line

sew to neck edge

Sew hood to neck of coat, right sides together, starting and finishing at the marks shown on the pattern.

5. Sew, preferably with a zigzag stitch, the seam allowances of hood/collar and coat to the top edges of the coat. Continue the line of sewing to the end of the neck, turning under the seam allowance of the top edges after the collar/hood ends. This holds everything together neatly and helps it to lie flat.

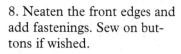
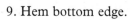

6. Neaten ends of sleeves.

7. Sew the underarm seams. Start at the end of the sleeve and finish at the hem.

8. Neaten the front edges and add fastenings. Sew on buttons if wished.

9. Hem bottom edge.

Variations

Jacket: Cut fronts and back shorter; for an anorak, sew in a zip at the centre front.

Pocket: The shape and position are shown on the pattern. Cut out and neaten all the edges. Sew onto the coat front, leaving the top edge open.

Shoes/Boots

These boots are a better fit on the jointed dolls than on the traditional ones. They are quick to make, especially if you use material that does not fray.

Fabric suggestions
Felt, soft suede or leather, polar fleece or tracksuit material.

Instructions

1. Cut out the pattern pieces. For a pair of boots you need 2 main pieces, cut from folded material, and 2 soles.

2. Cut a piece of narrow elastic in the length required for the size you are making:

large	$3^{1}/_{2}$ " (8cm)
medium	3 " (7cm)
small	$2^{1}/_{2}$ " (6cm)

Sew at ankle, on the wrong side, on the line marked. Stretch the elastic to fit the fabric at the ankle and sew as described for the direct application method.

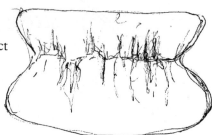

3. Fold the boot with wrong sides together and sew the centre front seam.

4. Sew sole to upper, matching the centre front and centre back as indicated on the pattern.

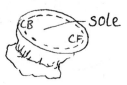

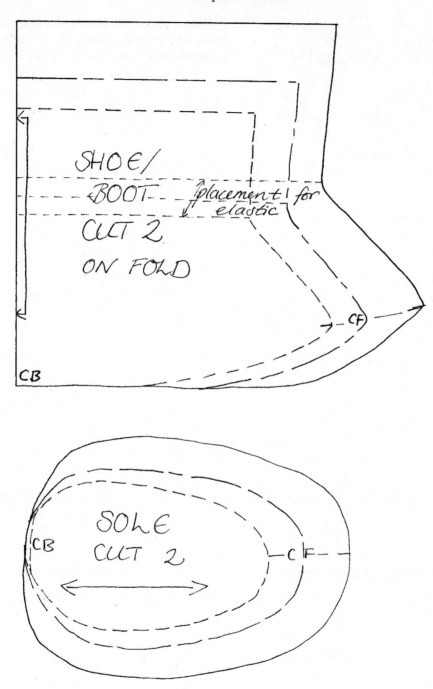

SHOE/
BOOT
CUT 2
ON FOLD

placement for elastic

CF

CB

SOLE
CUT 2

CB

C F

5. Turn under ¹/₂″ (1cm) at the top and sew down to finish the top of the boot.

6. Repeat to make the second boot.

Ballerina

A beautiful little dress
that turns any doll
into a dancer.
You can com-
plete the outfit by
making pretty
panties to match
and sewing tiny paper or silk
flowers onto ribbon to make a head dress.

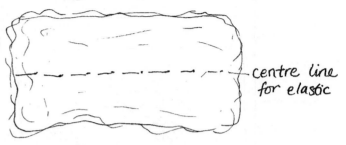

centre line for elastic

Fabric suggestions
Top: satin, silk, lightweight knitted material.
Skirt: dress net.

Instructions

1. Adapt the vest pattern (page 130) in the
appropriate size by shortening the body by 1″
(2.5cm), cutting the front neck lower and cutting the back open on the fold line.

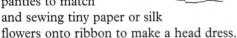

lower front neck

Shorten

2. Cut out the top using the
altered pattern. You should have 1
front and 2 backs.

cut open at centre back

3. Sew the side seams
and the shoulder seams.

shoulder seams

4. Neaten the armholes
and the neckline.

5. Neaten the back open-
ing and add fastenings.

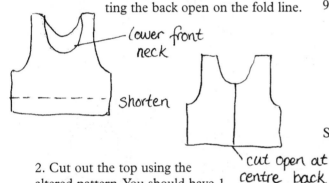

side seams

6. **Skirt**: Cut rectangles from dress net according to the instructions below:

large   3 pieces each 30″ x 12″ (75cm x 30cm)
medium 2 pieces each 25″ x 10″ (60cm x 25cm)
small   2 pieces each 20″ x 8″ (50cm x 20cm)

7. Make a pile of the pieces, aligning the edges.
Mark, with pins, the centre line along the
length of the net.

8. Measure the waist of the doll and add 1″
(2.5cm). Mark off this length on a piece of ¹/₂″
(1cm) wide elastic. Using the direct application
method, and stretching elastic to fit, sew the
elastic to the net on the marked line.

9. Fold skirt in half with the elastic inside.

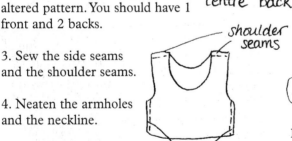

fold skirt in half

Sew the folded edge to the lower part of the
top, stretching the skirt to fit at the waist.

waist seam

10. Trim lower edge of net if necessary; there is
no need to hem, as net does not fray.

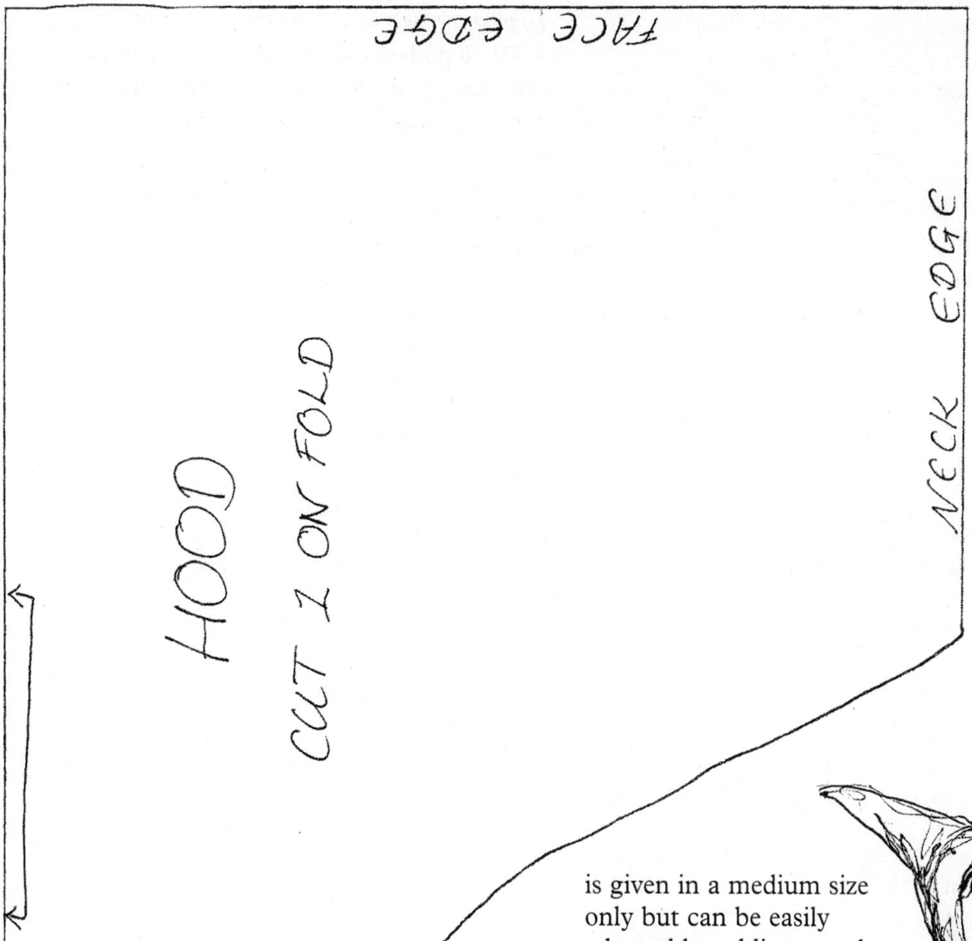

FACE EDGE

HOOD

CUT 1 ON FOLD

NECK EDGE

is given in a medium size only but can be easily adapted by adding or subtracting a little from the front and bottom edges of the hood and redrawing the semi-circle shape of the cape to fit the lower edge of the hood.

Woodland elf

Colour is most important for this outfit: browns and oranges suggest autumn in the forest and greens and yellows make us think of springtime. The cloak alone will be sufficient for most children but you can make a complete outfit by adding trousers or skirt and tabard (see soft dolls) in a toning colour to be worn over a plain top. The pattern

Fabric suggestions

Medium weight cotton or wool, tracksuit material. Felt can be used; it cannot be washed, but makes the cloak quick to make, as no hems are needed.

You also need narrow ribbon or braid for ties.

WOODLAND
ELF
CAPE

CUT 1 ON FOLD

Extend length as required

Instructions

1. Trace patterns for hood and cape. Complete the cape pattern by extending the lines to the length required. The shape is basically that of a half circle.

2. Cut out, from folded material, 1 hood and 1 cape.

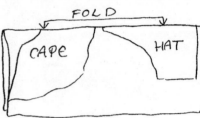

FOLD

CAPE   HAT

3. Sew back seam of hood.

sew
back
seam

4. Sew hood to neck of cape, stretching to fit where necessary.

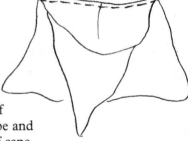

neck seam

5. Neaten front edges of hood and cape and lower edge of cape.

6. Sew on ties at neck edge. Each tie needs to be 12 - 14″ (30 - 35cm) long.

Other outfits

These are all based on patterns in this chapter; it is the colour and texture of the fabrics and trimmings that make them special.

Princess

Dress: Use the nightdress pattern to make a long dress in a beautiful silky material. Add lace or other trimmings to give a glamorous touch. You can omit the elastic at the wrists and widen the sleeves (see African dress below) to give a different style.

Cloak: Use the hood pattern from the coat and a rectangle of fabric, gathered on one long side, for the cloak itself. Follow the instructions for the Woodland Elf's cloak. Make the cloak from velvet or other rich fabric, perhaps trimmed with a fancy braid or fur fabric.

Accessories: She can have a necklace made from tiny beads and a simple crown of gold card. A more elaborate head dress can be made by measuring the doll's head and cutting a piece of elastic to fit. Cover the elastic with fabric or ribbon, sew into a circle, and attach a long train or veil of some soft material, such as chiffon or muslin.

Prince

Top: Make as for top and add some lace down the front or adapt the top to make a shirt.

Cloak: Make as for princess.

Trousers: Use the pattern given but make from velvet or brocade.

Accessories: Boots, in a dark colour, and a circle of metallic braid or card for a crown.

African dress

It is most important to find the right fabric for this dress. Look for an ethnic print, a piece of batik or handmade cottons in a colour to suit the doll.

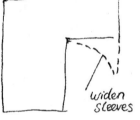

Extend the top pattern to make a long dress and widen the sleeves as shown in the diagram. Make up as for the top but with an opening at the front.

Style the doll's hair by making lots of tiny plaits and threading small beads onto the ends.

Sari outfit

Make a short sleeved top and long skirt in a plain colour to fit your doll.

Choose the fabric with care; the sari needs to have a border print or other strong pattern that is in scale with the doll, and the material must drape easily. A long Indian silk scarf would be ideal. No exact measurements are given as the method can be adapted to use varying quantities of fabric by adding or subtracting a few more tucks and pleats.

Take a rectangle of soft fabric and, starting at the back, tuck into the waist of the skirt. Continue to work round the doll, tucking the fabric into the waist of the skirt as you go. Traditionally there are a series of pleats at the centre front, but this is not essential, just make the waist look as neat as you can. Take the fabric right around the doll, ending at the front, the loose end is then taken over the left shoulder and left to hang free. You can secure the loose end, either by tucking into the waist at the back or by sewing on ribbon ties at the bottom corner, these are then tied at the front and hidden under the skirt.

Beds from baskets

A basket makes a good bed for a doll. A shallow shopping basket with a handle can be fitted out with bedding and provides a simple, mobile container for a favourite doll. The basket needs to be about 2″ (5cm) wider and longer than the doll itself.

Use a piece of paper, cut to fit the base of the basket, as a pattern for the bedding.

Mattress: Cut two pieces of fabric 1″ (2.5cm) larger all round than the pattern. Sew with right sides together, leaving a gap for turning and stuffing. Turn and stuff with sheepswool. Sew up the gap.

Pillow: Use the top third of the basic pattern to make a pattern for the pillow. Make as for the mattress.

Duvet: Use the bottom two thirds of the pattern to make a pattern for the duvet. Add 2 - 3″ (5 - 7cm) all round. Make as for the mattress.

duvet — pillow

Sheets and blankets: Cut rectangles of an appropriate size from cotton and wool fabrics. Turn under all the raw edges and hem. Sheets can be decorated with a little embroidery across the top edges and the woollen material can be edged with blanket stitch in a contrasting colour.

Carrycot

Materials
Quilted fabric –
for size see below
Firm ribbon or
braid: 1″ wide x 2m
Sewing thread to match
ribbon
1m cotton fabric to make bedding
Cardboard (*optional*)

large	16″ x 10″ (40cm x 25cm)
medium	14″ x 8″ (35cm x 20cm)
small	12″x 7″ (30cm x 17.5cm)

The carrycot is made entirely from fabric. It can be made from double-sided ready quilted fabric or you can make your own quilted fabric.

To quilt fabric: Cut 3 rectangles, 2 of fabric and 1 of polyester wadding or woven blanket fabric about 3″ (8cm) larger than the final size required.

Make a sandwich of the 3 layers, with the wadding in the centre. Tack or baste all three layers together.

fabric
polyester
wadding

Sew a line of stitches about ¹/₂″ (1cm) from one edge.

Sew further lines of stitches 1″ (2.5cm) apart to cover the entire piece of fabric.

Trim edges and use to make the fabric to make the carrycot.

To make the carrycot
1. Cut a rectangle from quilted fabric in the appropriate size:

large	26″ x 20″ (65cm x 50cm)
medium	22″ x 16″ (55cm x 40cm)
small	18″ x 13″ (45cm x 32.5cm)

2. Cut a square of fabric from each corner:

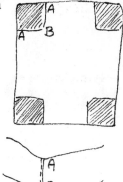

large	5″ (12.5cm)
medium	4″ (10cm)
small	3″ (7.5cm)

3. Sew the inner edges of the square together. Match A to A and sew from A to B to make the corner.

4. Fold ribbon over the raw edges at the top of the car-rycot. Pin or tack to hold in place. Sew through all layers.

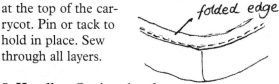

folded edge

5. **Handles**: Cut lengths of ribbon as indicated:

large	2 x 20″ (50cm)
medium	2 x 18″ (45cm)
small	2 x 16″ (40cm)

Divide the long side of the carrycot into three equal parts and sew the handles 3″ (7.5cm) onto the centre third, following the diagram.

6. *Optional*: place cardboard in the bottom of the carrycot.

Bedding

All the sizes stated for bedding include ½″ (1cm) seam allowances.

Mattress
Cut 2 rectangles according to the measurements below:

large	17″ x 11″ (42.5cm x 27.5cm)
medium	15″ x 9″ (37.5cm x 22.5cm)
small	13″ x 8″ (32.5cm x 20cm)

Sew with right sides together, leaving a gap on one long side. At each corner, match adjoining seams and sew across the resulting triangle about 1½″ (3cm) from the end.

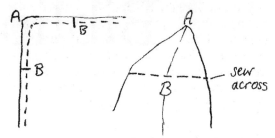

sew across

Trim the corners and turn the mattress cover. Stuff with sheepswool. Sew up the gap by hand.

Pillow
Cut 2 rectangles according to the measurements below:

large	11″ x 5″ (27.5cm x 12.5cm)
medium	9″ x 4½″ (22.5cm x 11.25cm)
small	8″ x 4″ (20cm x 10cm)

Sew with right sides together, leaving a gap for turning and stuffing. Turn and stuff with sheepswool. Sew up the gap by hand.

Duvet
Cut 2 squares according to the measurements below:

large	14″ x 14″ (35cm x 35cm)
medium	12″ x 12″ (30cm x 30cm)
small	11″ x 11″ (27.5cm x 27.5cm)

Sew with right sides together, leaving a gap for turning and stuffing. Turn and stuff with sheepswool. Sew up the gap by hand.

Sheets and blankets
Follow the instructions given for beds made from baskets.

Bibliography

Lois Cusick   *Waldorf Parenting Handbook*
St George Publications (via Rudolf
Steiner Press) 1979

Theo Gimble   *The Book of Colour Healing*
Gaia Books 1994

Caroline von Heydebrand   *Childhood*
Anthroposophical Press 1995

Mary Hillier   *Dolls and Dollmaking*
Weidenfeld & Nicolson 1968

Gladys Meyer   *The Mystery Wisdom of Colour*
New Knowledge Books 1961

Joan Salter   *The Incarnating Child*
Hawthorn Press 1987

Lia van Steenderen   *Dolls and Dolls Clothes*
Exeley Publications Ltd 1987

Rudolf Steiner et al   *Education as an Art*
Rudolf Steiner Press 1970
(especially the lecture 'The Child at
Play' by Caroline von Heydebrand)

Michael Wilson *What is Colour – A Goethean
Approach*   Goethean Science
Foundation 1949

Suppliers

United Kingdom

John Lewis – to find your nearest branch
contact:
John Lewis
Oxford Street
London W1A 1EX
Telephone: +(44) (0)20 7629 7711
E-mail: jl_oxford_street@johnlewis.co.uk
www.johnlewis.com/index.asp

Stockinette (sold from the Haberdashery
Dept.).
All general sewing supplies, fabrics and knitting
wools.

Fabric Land
Head Office
Silver Business Park
Airfield Way
Christchurch
Dorset BH23 3TA
Telephone: +(44) (0)1202 480802

General sewing supplies and fabric (including
velour).

Dainty Supplies Ltd
Unit 35 Phoenix Road
Crowther Industrial Estate
District 3
Washington
Tyne & Wear NE38 OAD
Telephone: +(44) (0)191 416 886

Good mail order source of stockinette and
other craft supplies.

Texere Yarns
College Mill
Barkerend Road
Bradford BD1 4AU

Telephone: +(44) (0)1274 722191
www.texere-yarns.co.uk
enquiries@texere-yarns.co.uk

Mail order. Knitting yarns of all descriptions.

Wool Marketing Board
British Wool Marketing Board
Wool House
Roydsdale Way
Euroway Trading Est.
Bradford
West Yorkshire BD4 6SE
Telephone: +(44) (0)1274 688666
Fax: +(44) (0)1274 652233
traceyhardisty@britishwool.org.uk>

Sheep fleece.

Boots the Chemist – to find your nearest
branch contact
Boots The Chemists Limited
PO Box 5300
Nottingham NG90 1AA
Telephone:
United Kingdom +(44) (0)845 070 8090
Republic of Ireland +(353) (0)1890 708091
www.boots.co.uk/
Email btc.cshelpdesk@boots.co.uk

Finger bandage in stock, will order other sizes
of cotton bandage.

My Favourite Things
53 Salisbury Road
Redland
Bristol BS6 7AS
Telephone: +(44) (0)117 924 3577
Kinderdolls@hotmail.com

Carded sheepswool, stockinette and other doll-making supplies.
Kits to make some of the dolls from this book.

USA

Magic Cabin Dolls
Magic Cabin Processing Center
1950 Waldorf NW
Grand Rapids, MI 49550-7000
Telephone: +(1) 888 623 3655
www.magiccabindolls.com

Carded sheepswool, cotton knit, dollmaking supplies and much, much more.

Weir Dolls
2909 Parkridge Drive
Ann Arbor
MI 48103-1734
Telephone: +(1)734 668 6992
           or +(1)888 205 5034
weirdoll@provide.net
www.weirdolls.com

Dollmaking supplies, including cotton knit fabric.

Australia

Winterwood Steiner Inspired Toys
PO Box 4034 Croydon Hills
Victoria 3134
Australia
Phone +(61) (0)39872 4729
Fax +(61) (0)39872 4944
E mail address winterwood@bigpond.com.au

Dollmaking supplies, including cotton knit fabric.

Other books from Hawthorn Press

Muddles, Puddles and Sunshine
Your activity book to help when someone has died
Winston's Wish

Muddles, Puddles and Sunshine offers practical and sensitive support for bereaved children. Beautifully illustrated in colour, it suggests a helpful series of activities and exercises accompanied by the friendly characters of Bee and Bear.

32pp; 297 x 210mm landscape; paperback;
1 869 890 58 2

Helping Children to Overcome Fear
The healing power of play
Russell Evans

Critical illness can cause overwhelming feelings of abandonment and loss. Difficult for adults to face alone, for children the experience is magnified. They have to leave home for an alien hospital world, without the comfort of familiar daily rhythms. Jean Evans was a play leader who recognised ahead of her time the importance of enabling children to give voice to their feelings, providing opportunities for play and working in partnership with parents. These requirements are now core principles in the training and working practice in the fields of nursery nursing, play therapy, childcare and Paediatrics.

Early Years Series; 128pp; 216 x 138mm; paperback;
1 903458 02 1

The Future of Childhood
Edited by Christopher Clouder, Sally Jenkinson and Martin Large

Children create our future with their gifts and talents, yet what does childhood mean for us today? Is childhood vanishing under the impact of poverty, commercialism, stress, social breakdown and hot housing? And, given such threats to childhood, how can we create a healthy world for bringing up children? The *Alliance for Childhood* is a forum where individuals and organisations can work together out of respect for childhood, in a world-wide effort to improve children's lives. This lively collection of articles by presenters at their Brussels Conference in August 2000 offers stimulating insight for dialogue about how we can give due respect to children. Included are useful references, contacts and resources for networking.

Early Years Series;
176pp; 216 x 138mm; paperback;
1 903458 10 2

Storytelling with Children
Nancy Mellon

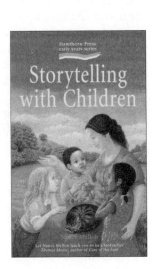

Telling stories awakens wonder and creates special occasions with children, whether it is bedtime, around the fire or on rainy days. Encouraging you to spin golden tales, Nancy Mellon shows how you can become a confident storyteller and enrich your family with the power of story. Children love family storytelling and parents can learn this practical, magical art.

Here are tips and resources you need for:

- Creating a listening space
- Using the day's events and rhythms to make stories
- Transforming old stories and making up new ones
- Bringing your personal and family stories to life
- Learning stories by heart using pictures, inner theatre, walk-about, singing the story and other methods
- Finding the tale you want from her rich story-cupboard.

Early Years Series;
192pp; 216 x 138mm; illustrations; paperback;
1 903458 08 0

Games Children Play
How games and sport help children develop
Kim Brooking-Payne
Illustrated by Marije Rowling

Games Children Play offers an accessible guide to games with children of age 3 upwards. These games are all tried and tested, and are the basis for the author's extensive teacher training work. The book explores children's personal development and how this is expressed in movement, play, songs and games.

Each game is clearly and simply described, with diagrams or drawings, and accompanied by an explanation of why this game is helpful at a particular age. The equipment that may be needed is basic, cheap and easily available.

192pp; 297 x 210mm; paperback;
1 869 890 78 7

Free Range Education
Ed Terri Dowty

Considering educating your children at home? Then *Free Range Education* will help you make better choices by asking 'what is home education?', 'what are the benefits?', and 'how do you educate at home?' Parents and students describe their approaches to education at home and provide helpful examples, good stories, resources, contacts and information on your rights.

256pp; 210 x 148mm; paperback; cartoons;
1 903 458 07 2

Free to Learn
Introducing Steiner Waldorf early years education
Lynne Oldfield

'… the early years are not a phase of life to be rushed through, but a stage of tremendous importance needing to be experienced fully in its own right. Underpinning this book is the conviction that the child's early learning is profound; that quality of early experience is every bit as important as quantity. …'

(From the Foreword by Sally Jenkinson)

Early Years Series; 160pp; 216 x 138mm; paperback;
1 903458 06 4

Pull the Other One!
String Games and Stories Book 1
Michael Taylor

This well-travelled and entertaining series of tales is accompanied by clear instructions and explanatory diagrams – guaranteed not to tie you in knots and will teach you tricks with which to dazzle your friends! With something for everyone, these ingenious tricks and tales are developed and taught with utter simplicity, making them suitable from age 5 upwards.

'When we go wrong playing Cat's Cradle, we call it Dog's Cradle!'
(Megan Gain, aged 6, London)

Storytelling Series;
128pp; 216 x 148mm; drawings; paperback;
1 869 890 49 3

Naming
Choosing a meaningful name
Caroline Sherwood

'Caroline Sherwood's *Naming* is a completely new and far more useful approach in which the meanings of names are the prime focus. With a deep respect for language, she offers a fresh way for parents to set about finding the right name for their child.'
(Rosie Styles, The Baby Naming Society)

304pp; 246 x 189mm; paperback;
1 869 890 56 6

The Genius of Play
Sally Jenkinson

This book is an observation of the tireless imagination of the child when it is allowed to develop naturally, and how this shapes the perceptions of the later adult. It addresses what 'play' is, why it is necessary and its modern difficulties.

Early Years Series;
128pp; 216 x 138; paperback;
1 903458 04 8

Being a Parent
Parent Network

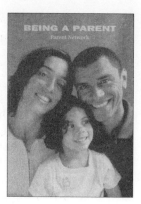

Being a Parent helps you think about what support you and your children need. It gives ideas on how to make family life a little easier.

'I consider this book and other Parent Network courses to have great value, because I believe that parents deserve all the help they can get...'
 Alan Titchmarsh, TV and Radio Broadcaster, Author and Gardener

96pp; 297 x 210mm; paperback;
1 869 890 81 7

Parenting Matters
Ways to bring up your children using heart and head
Parent Network

Parenting Matters helps you bring up loving and happy children. Here is the heart to becoming the more confident, sensitive, relaxed, firm and caring parent that you truly are – enjoying your children and family.

'... a chance to sort out your thinking and raise your kids in the way you really want to, instead of in a series of knee-jerk reactions.'
 (Steve Biddulph, family therapist and parenting author)

228pp; 297 x 210mm; paperback;
1 869 890 16 7

Four books in the Crafts, Festivals and Family Activities Series:

All Year Round
Ann Druitt, Christine Fynes-Clinton, Marije Rowling

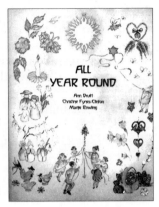

All Year Round is brimming with things to make; activities, stories, poems and songs to share with your family. It is full of well-illustrated ideas for fun and celebration: from Candlemas to Christmas and Midsummer's day to the Winter solstice. Observing the round of festivals is an enjoyable way to bring rhythm into children's lives and provide a series of meaningful landmarks to look forward to.

Each festival has a special character of its own: participation can deepen our understanding and love of nature and bring a gift to the whole family.

288pp; 250 x 200mm; paperback;
1 869 890 47 7

Festivals, Family and Food
Diana Carey and Judy Large

A source of stories, recipes, things to make, activities, poems, songs and festivals. Each festival such as Christmas, Candlemas and Martinmas has its own, well-illustrated chapter.

There are also sections on Birthdays, Rainy Days, Convalescence and a birthday Calendar. The perfect present for a family, it explores the numerous festivals that children love celebrating.

'It's an invaluable resource book'   (*The Observer*)

'Every family should have one'   (*Daily Mail*)

216pp; 250 x 200mm; illustrations; paperback; 0 950 706 23 X

Festivals Together
A guide to multicultural celebration
Sue Fitzjohn, Minda Weston, Judy Large

This special book for families and teachers helps you celebrate festivals from cultures from all over the world. This resource guide for celebration introduces a selection of 26 Buddhist, Christian, Hindu, Jewish, Muslim and Sikh festivals. It offers a lively introduction to the wealth of different ways of life. There are stories, things to make, recipes, songs, customs and activities for each festival, comprehensively illustrated.

'The ideal book for anyone who wants to tackle multicultural festivals.'
(Nursery World)

224pp; 250 x 200mm; paperback;
1 869 890 46 9

The Children's Year
Crafts and clothes for children and parents to make
Stephanie Cooper, Christine Fynes-Clinton, Marije Rowling

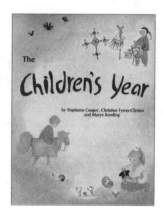

You needn't be an experienced craftsperson to create beautiful things! This step by step, well-illustrated book with clear instructions shows you how to get started. Children and parents are encouraged to try all sorts of handwork, with different projects relating to the seasons of the year.

Here are soft toys, wooden toys, moving toys such as balancing birds or climbing gnomes, horses, woolly hats, mobiles and dolls. There are over 100 treasures to make in seasonal groupings around the children's year.

192pp; 250 x 200mm; paperback;
1 869 890 00 0

If you have difficulties ordering Hawthorn Press books from a book-shop, you can order direct from:

Scottish Book Source Distribution
137 Dundee Street
Edinburgh, EH11 1BG

Tel: +(44) (0)131 229 6800
Fax: +(44) (0)131 229 9070

For further information or a book catalogue, please contact:

Hawthorn Press
Hawthorn House
1 Lansdown Lane
Stroud
Gloucestershire GL5 1BJ

Tel: +(44) (0)1453 757040
Fax: +(44) (0)1453 751138
E-mail: info@hawthornpress.com
Website: www.hawthornpress.com